MW01244785

Climbing Up

*Preparing on the Inside for
Service on the Outside*

Climbing Up: Preparing on the Inside for Service on the Outside
© 2020. Completion Global, Inc. All Rights Reserved

Copying, redistribution and/or sale of these materials, or any
unauthorized transmission, except as may be expressly permitted by
the 1976 Copyright Act or in writing from the publisher is prohibited.
Requests for permission should be addressed in writing to:
Completion Global, Inc., 4261 E. University Avenue, #337, Prosper,
TX 75078.

ISBN: 978-1-7354848-0-8 (print)
ISBN: 978-1-7354848-1-5 (digital)

Scripture quotations are from the ESV® Bible (The Holy Bible, English
Standard Version®), copyright © 2001 by Crossway, a publishing ministry
of Good News Publishers. Used by permission. All rights reserved.

Dedication

To Mark Walker and Quentin Valdois of *The Cell Church*. Thank you for encouraging us to write this book, for being patient with our many questions, and for your instruction out of the wealth of your expertise.

Acknowledgements

Thanks to Dillon for your inspiration and input in the crafting of *Climbing Up*. The excellence of your walk with Christ and your preparation for release is what motivated us to get this done. To Charles Anderson, we are grateful for the word of encouragement you gave us in 2019, that this book would be used of God in a significant way to help prisoners and their families. To Mary Flin and Matt Thomas, thanks for your expertise and counsel. To Rich Esselstrom, thanks for helping us collect source materials and for your work in California to empower urban leaders and former prisoners. To Harold Roesler, we appreciate your help in the editing and publishing process, and your service as Chairman of the Board of *Completion Global*.

Table of Contents

Appendices

Foreword

As CEO of Kairos Prison Ministry International, I've heard a lot of your stories directly and from our Kairos volunteers. We hear of the struggles and the good times you and your family had, and are having, while you are in prison. As I have worked with Don and Cathy Allsman on the board of Correctional Ministry and Chaplains Association, I am impressed of their love for our Lord and passion to serve and to provide support to those incarcerated, especially as they are getting out.

We all know the process of enculturation while in prison has taken place. One of the most important things you can do is recognize that, understand it, and know how to deal with it overall.

In your life, it is not the end, it's the beginning. You're getting out soon. Time for a new start and for you to be the person you know God has called you to be. But time did not stand still while you were in prison. Family, society, communities, technology, and all aspects of the world progressed forward and changed. While you were inside, the world outside moved. It's up to you to know how you've changed and how your family and society has changed so you fit in and succeed in your re-entry into the local culture and society.

In *Climbing Up*, Don and Cathy help you prepare to think how you have changed while in prison and why, how your family and friends may have changed and why, how living in your community has changed and why, and how to be successful in embracing life outside the prison walls. Understanding yourself and your surroundings was critical in prison. Now you're getting out, so you will have to be understanding and patient as you adapt to the numerous changes in yourself and the society around you.

It's up to you to address, as others cannot do it for you, and *Climbing Up* gives you great insight into culture, church, and people dynamics

Climbing Up

you need to understand and think about. This book will help you face the reality of where you are now and what to prepare for as you go home.

You may not want to hear some of the important points made in *Climbing Up* but you need to hear them, process them, and understand them to be successful in your re-entry to society. Dig deep into the messages shared so as you are Climbing Up you can approach the outside world with clarity and realistic expectations.

Know who you are in Christ, be true to yourself and God, and as shared in this book, understand your identity is in Christ. Read *Climbing Up* carefully and slowly. Stop and think through the messages and the questions in every chapter. And in the end, prepare a plan such as the 3-3-3-12 approach they explain.

Make sure you are planning what you expect of yourself and not setting yourself up for disappointment by expecting special things of others. And learn so you adapt your plan as you go, facing situations while staying true to Jesus Christ. Now that re-entry is a reality, use your resources well. Don and Cathy's *Climbing Up* will help you prepare and succeed.

We are praying for your success. God loves you and wants you to be successful so lean on Him at all times. Trust Him and trust yourself to be the Christ-centered person God is preparing you to be. Don't believe the lie, "You can't make it." Trust in the truth, Jesus Christ, and you can succeed. Take it step by step with the Lord as you are Climbing Up.

Evelyn Lemly
CEO, Kairos Prison Ministry International, Inc.

Introduction

You have been down for years, but now you look forward to going home! As the time draws near for release, you may feel joyful anticipation or a gnawing feeling of apprehension (or some of both).

You may have attended classes to take advantage of opportunities to grow into an effective leader, or you may have been just counting down the time through hobbies, watching TV, reading, or writing poetry. In either case, now is the time to prepare for re-entry, Climbing Up from incarceration, a new season of freedom on the outside.

Expectations

American society has low expectations for returning citizens. Some view the incarcerated with contempt or pity, believing they are morally bankrupt or intellectually incompetent. Their highest aspiration for someone returning to society is to somehow become a law-abiding citizen and not return to prison.

But we wrote this book because we have much higher expectations of you than simply avoiding re-incarceration. We believe you can be an asset to your community, a highly prized person who makes significant contributions in the world. Consequently, this book is for those who desire to exceed expectations, for those who want to make a substantial impact for good.

We believe that God has placed within you a deep desire to be significant, to make a difference, to *be* somebody. But this will require hard work. Being down has affected you in ways that you are not even aware. If you apply yourself to Climbing Up during this time leading up to your release, you will be in a good position to succeed.

Climbing Up

If you think you can magically change the moment you step through the gate, you are in for a rude awakening. So instead of immersing yourself in musings about your future, you can spend this time proactively preparing for your release.

The Fundamentals

The secret to success in any area of life is mastery of the fundamentals. This is true in music, sports, business, and academics. When Don was a teenager, he had the opportunity to attend John Wooden's basketball camp during the last part of UCLA's historic string of nine NCAA championships in 12 years.

Don learned that success in basketball, even for talented All-Americans, was a result of mastering the fundamentals. When Don was old enough to coach our son and his friends, he followed Coach Wooden's philosophy by teaching them the basics.

Climbing Up addresses the fundamentals of re-entry, and if you prepare yourself on the inside, you will be equipped to be a servant of Christ on the outside. You will not only <u>survive</u> in the free world; you will <u>thrive</u> by mastering three fundamental skills:

Part I: Recognize the Culture

Every family, every village, and every society follows a set of rules to ensure a good life in their context. To thrive in any given place, you must comply with the unspoken rules of that culture. Each place has its own expectations of behavior, that if violated, will result in pain, hardship, even death. This is true of prison, as well as life on the outside (aka civilian life). If you are unaware of these differences, you will walk into awkward and difficult situations without knowing what is happening. **This section will show how you have been** shaped by prison culture, and how it differs from the culture of civilian life.

Part II: Remember Your Identity

If you are a follower of Jesus, you have experienced His power that transformed you from the person you were, to become the person you are destined to be. God has equipped you to be forged into the image of Christ, taking a new identity as His ambassador. But the challenges of re-entry can be so daunting, you will be susceptible to forgetting your identity in Christ. When you find yourself in these difficult situations, you need the ability to draw upon the strength of who you are as His Kingdom warrior. **This section will give you practical tools to remember your identity in Christ every day.**

Part III: Adapt to Win

While it is vital to prepare for life on the outside, you will find that re-entry will be full of surprises, disappointments, and setbacks. It is common for prisoners to make very detailed plans only to see several parts of their plans go up in smoke shortly after release. While recognizing cultural differences and remembering your identity are important, you will also need this third skill to succeed in re-entry: the ability to revise your plans. In other words, you must adapt to win. **This section will equip you by exploring a real-life adventure into the unknown that required adaptability but resulted in tremendous success.**

Instructions

At the end of each chapter, there are questions to help you process the content. These are extremely important for your re-entry because they force you slow down and incorporate the lessons of that chapter before you move ahead. Do not rush through the book.

Also, complete these exercises in a separate notebook so you can use as many pages as you need. That way, you can share this book with others without disclosing confidential thoughts written in the margins.

The Appendices contain essential information. Some will be referenced as you proceed through the chapters and others can be read after the completion of Part III. Some of the appendices are important for foundational understanding. For example, references to books of the Bible are abbreviated in the book, so if you are not familiar with a reference see Appendix 10. If you are not a follower of Christ or do now know what that means, see Appendix 7. Make sure you read carefully through each Appendix to get the maximum benefit from this book.

A Word of Warning

In our years of conversations with returning citizens from all over America, their experiences have been consistent, giving us confidence to advise you about your re-entry journey. While acknowledging that a few things in the book may not apply to your situation, we also know your tendency will be to ignore our counsel because it is difficult to hear.

For example, after giving our friend Dillon an early draft of this book, he shared some of our claims with his fellow inmates and reported, "We experienced dissonance as a result of the clash between our estimations of reality and a conflicting estimation from Don and Cathy, who have more knowledge and experience on the subject of re-entry and purposeful living. We were tempted to ignore or dismiss their claims in an attempt to resolve the negative emotions we experienced from them."

But he went on to say, "What will we choose to believe: our own biased, uninformed, and potentially unrealistic estimation of the process of re-entry, or the objective, informed, and realistic estimation of men and women who love us, desire to see us accomplish God's will for our lives, and have sacrificed to produce this resource to help us toward that end?"

Dillon speaks to you when he warns, "Instead of saying, 'these people don't know me and are claiming I have problems,' when you read *Climbing Up*, recognize your discomfort, pause to process your negative response, acknowledge your reaction might be due to an unrealistic estimation of your own thinking, and get lined up with objective reality as it is. Own it! My challenge and plea is for you to be ruthlessly honest with yourself and strive to be as objective as possible in your self-assessment as you read this material."

<u>Your Family and Friends</u>

There is another group of people who can benefit from this book: your family and friends on the outside. You cannot successfully climb up alone; you need the help of others to attain a life of effective service in civilian culture. Although they will not fully understand what you have been through in prison, this book will give them a place to start so they can assist you in your journey.

<u>The Stakes are High</u>

Your success in Climbing Up is important, not just for you, but also for those who re-enter after you. If you provide a good example of someone coming out of prison, those on the outside will be more willing to take a chance on other returning citizens in the future. But if you mess up, it will cause the outside world to be more cynical about the credibility of those being released.

Climbing Up

You do not have to be perfect, but you need to be sober about your responsibilities to the Lord Jesus, yourself, your loved ones, and the brothers and sisters looking to you to pave the way for their future.

This book is not just for you, but for untold people waiting to be blessed by you. Just think what refreshment awaits the people in your world if you become a powerful force for good. You can do it! The Lord is with you and there are people who believe in you!

We pray that you will allow God to do His work of producing abundant fruit through your life. You have been down at the bottom, but it is time to start Climbing Up!

Part I: Recognize the Culture

"Toto, I've a feeling we're not in Kansas anymore."

- Dorothy, The Wizard of Oz

———————————

Chapter 1
Culture Eats Strategy for Breakfast

CATHY MOVED A LOT growing up, living in different parts of the country. She knew the importance of learning how to fit in each time she was the new kid at school. In order to have a good life, she had to discover what to wear, who the key people were, how to talk with the right accent, and what the important topics of conversation were. No one sat her down to explain these rules. She had to learn them by observation. Failure to acclimate quickly to the unspoken rules of behavior in each location made it difficult, if not impossible, to thrive in her new life.

The set of unspoken rules about behavior is called "culture."

Culture is a pattern of behavior, often expressed in terms of preferences for food, language, clothes, and a sense of what is beautiful (or repulsive). Your family had preferences, and so did the community where you grew up. If you want to enjoy a good life in any given place, you must learn to conform to their culture. Conversely, if you violate the culture you will be punished, resulting in suffering or sometimes even death. This is true in prison, as well as life on the outside.

Right, Wrong, or Neutral

From God's point of view, no culture is purely good and no culture is purely evil. Cultures have elements that promote godly actions, other aspects that encourage sin, but mostly are simply preferences that are neither right nor wrong. For example, there is no single "Christian" food, language, or clothing style. God delights in the diversity of His creation as it is expressed in all its variety around the world.

Climbing Up

In America, there are cultural elements that are good (e.g. a strong work ethic), some that encourage evil (e.g. tendency toward greed), but most are neither good nor bad (e.g. preferences for hot dogs and apple pie).

Prison culture has virtuous elements (e.g. strong bonds of Christian fellowship), evil tendencies (e.g. acceptance of violence), but has many aspects that are neutral. Prison has its own language, its own economy, and a preference for treasured foods (the foods that are used for special occasions in your prison experience).

Culture Never Seems Neutral

The rules for experiencing a good life are taught to us as children and they become normal from a young age. Our understanding of what is good and beautiful starts before we can remember. These definitions about clothing, food, family, community, and music become the standard, and anyone who behaves differently will stick out as odd.

Because we learn culture from our families and communities in terms of "right and wrong," we put neutral actions in the "right or wrong" category. For example, if you learned that it was wrong to chew your food with your mouth open, any time you saw this behavior, you would find it repulsive. Or if a mom sees her child wearing colors that do not match, she will say, "That is wrong, go change your clothes." But from God's perspective these cultural rules are neutral.

Culture Is Invisible

It is nearly impossible for anyone to understand their own culture because it is invisible to them. For example, when Don was a teenager in the 70s, his family travelled to another country. As they were walking, people asked, "You are Americans, aren't you?" After this happened several times, Don asked, "How did you know?" They said, "Your tennies gave you away."

At that time in history only Americans wore tennis shoes (or tennies) in public. Nike's influence had not yet expanded around the world, and the appearance of white shoes for walking was outside the boundary of cultural normalcy. Don was identified as an American because no one in that culture would be found walking the streets in white running shoes. What was invisible to Don stuck out like a sore thumb in that culture.

There is a saying, "Fish discover water last." In other words, it is hard for fish to realize they are in water because it is their natural habitat. Culture is to us as water is to fish; it is the natural habitat in which we live. So we do not tend to even notice our own culture. For example, in the U.S., a friendly parting expression is, "Have a nice day!" But in other cultures, this is offensive and they may say, "Who gives her the right to tell me what kind of day I must have?"

Therefore, while your cultural preferences can easily be recognized by others, you cannot see them in yourself. They are invisible, like the air you breathe. In fact, if you want to understand your own culture, ask someone from a different culture to describe yours. While they may report some annoying exaggerations, you are likely to receive interesting insights you never noticed before.

In the same way, the culture of prison is invisible to you. From the day of arrival you were taught the acceptable rules of behavior and have been quietly adapting ever since. Although it was difficult to acclimate at first, you developed friends in this culture, found significance in this culture, and have grown in your faith in this culture. The longer you have been in prison, the more normal those cultural rules became, and the more challenging it will be to adapt to a different culture upon release. This does not mean you enjoy being incarcerated; it simply means you have successfully adapted in your present culture.

Shifting Back is Difficult

Many returning citizens have reported how difficult it was to make the cultural transition because they did not even realize there was a cultural shift involved. Because prison culture was invisible to them, it was a shock to find out how enculturated they had become.

They believed if they studied the Bible and became a Christian leader in prison, it would guarantee them a smooth transition into civilian life. But flourishing as a Christian in one culture does make it easy to follow Christ in another. Scott Stroud watched prisoners attend Bible studies, work through 12-step programs, and lead others to Christ, but said, "The reality is they don't know the first thing about living as a Christian on the outside."[1]

Also, when you go back to free-world culture, it will not be the same as you remember it to be. Although you grew up in civilian culture, now you have been acclimated to prison culture, and going back will be a brand-new experience. For example, if someone grew up in Venezuela and then moved to Thailand, the longer they lived in Thailand, the less they would remember the rules of their Venezuelan childhood. And if they went back to Venezuela as an adult, they would find that life was different in Venezuela than they remembered as a youth.

How Weird Am I?

Other returning citizens report that they stepped into civilian life with full awareness that the culture would be different, but did not know what that would mean. Quentin Valdois of *The Cell Church* said, "Former prisoners know they are weird, but they don't know *how* they are weird." You may have the same fears: you know that your behaviors are different, but you do not know *why* they are different. You know you will do things on the outside that are culturally abnormal, but you do not know what that will look like.

As you are Climbing Up, it is imperative to learn the cultural differences between prison life and civilian life. We even go so far as to propose that **the primary reason people return to prison after release is a failure to adjust to civilian culture.** While many people believe it is a failure of *character*, we maintain it is a failure of *cultural* adjustment. Therefore, the first fundamental skill for you to develop is to recognize the cultural differences between prison and civilian culture.

Conclusion

Culture assumptions are powerful because they are invisible. In fact, the rules of behavior are basic to all human functioning everywhere people live. Culture is more powerful than your plans, more powerful than your effort, more powerful than your good intentions.

Business guru Peter Drucker is credited with the phrase, "Culture eats strategy for breakfast." In other words, the unspoken rules about how to behave are the most powerful forces in that community, and no cleverly devised strategy can nullify it. Culture is at the top of the food chain. Culture eats strategy for breakfast.

Climbing Up

Questions for Reflection

Think about where you grew up and reflect on the unspoken rules of culture you adopted. In other words, what did you learn from your family or community about the following:

1. The Big Questions: What role did family play in your community? How was information exchanged? To be a success, what was important to achieve in life? What conditions were needed to have "the good life."

2. The Beauty Questions: What was good food versus bad food? What images or colors were pleasant and which ones ugly? What defined good clothing? What activities were important or fun? How were some emotions expressed and how were other emotions punished? How was art, stories, music, dance, or drama expressed?

3. The Idea Questions: What made an idea bad or good, right or wrong? What were the common religious beliefs? How did people buy and sell? What tools or technologies were used and valued? What was good politics versus evil politics?

Chapter 2
The Lessons of Culture

To MAKE A SUCCESSFUL transition into the free world, you need to recognize the invisible rules of prison culture because they influence the way you think and act. But first, a broader context of cultural differences in America and in Church history may be helpful.

For 30 years we served with World Impact, an inner-city missions organization dedicated to raising up leaders from America's urban poor in cities from Los Angeles to Newark, NJ. We began as volunteers in Wichita, Kansas and then later joined staff in Los Angeles. Over the years we learned a lot about culture, both from the people living in the inner city (primarily people of color) and the missionaries who moved in to serve in their neighborhoods (primarily Anglos).

American cities have a collection of various cultures and sub-cultures, interacting within a prevailing culture. The collection of immigrant and ethnic groups, each with their own aspirations and heritage, makes for complex situations. Some groups want to assimilate into the dominant culture, others want to retain their cultural heritage, and a third group may want to do both: assimilate but retain their culture. Trying to navigate these swirling waters is difficult, especially when the rules of culture are unspoken and invisible.

I Don't Fit In

In the 60s and 70s, World Impact missionaries led young Black people to Christ and brought them to the missionaries' suburban Anglo churches. Not surprisingly, the urban youth would express feelings of not fitting in, so the missionaries started taking them to nearby African-American churches. The assumption was that any Black church would be welcoming to any Black person.

Climbing Up

But our staff were puzzled when their young disciples said, "I don't fit there." How could young African Americans not feel accepted at churches full of other African Americans, in a church building right in their neighborhood?

When asked why, the common response was, "I don't have the right clothes; I don't understand what they are saying and doing; I don't know the songs; I don't have money for the offerings." These same conversations were taking place in every inner city where World Impact was ministering.

The mistake the missionaries were making was equating <u>culture</u> (unspoken rules of behavior) with <u>color</u> (the color of people's skin). In other words, being ethnically Black does not mean that all Black people share the same cultural preferences. After much reflection and dialogue, Dr. Keith Phillips, then president of World Impact, developed a paradigm describing American sub-culture in the inner city.[2] The reality was that each ethnic group had at least three separate sub-cultures existing at once, represented by the diagram below:

Interaction of Class, Culture, and Ethnicity

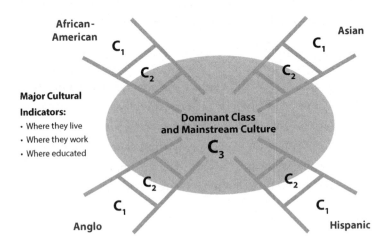

The Lessons of Culture

Explaining the Diagram

The prevailing culture, "Dominant Class and Mainstream Culture," in the middle of the diagram, is the benchmark for American culture. In some cases this has been referred to as "Anglo-Saxon-Protestant." The unspoken rules for what constitute a good American life are generated from this source, which is labeled "C_3." It is these cultural norms that exert the greatest influence on everyone who lives in the U.S.

This prevailing culture (C_3) is defined as being surrounded on three sides using these characteristics (see "Major Cultural Indicators"): 1) where a person lives; 2) where a person works; 3) where a person was educated. Within this mainstream, prevailing culture, there are several ethnic groups in America including African American, Asian, Hispanic, and Anglo (there are others but these four are used for illustration). Each of these four ethnic groups can be divided into three cultures, noted as C_1, C_2, and C_3.

Therefore, regardless of a person's heritage, whether it is African, Asian, Latin American, or European, where that person lives, works, and was educated are the determining factors that shape their cultural preferences in America.

African-American Examples

For example, a C_3 Black person lives in a predominantly Anglo neighborhood, works at company run mostly by White people, and was educated at colleges traditionally run by Caucasians. For example, Barak Obama lived in the Presidential Mansion, worked as the President of the United States, and was educated at Ivy League schools. Therefore, he was surrounded on all three sides by the dominant culture, even though he is ethnically Black.

Climbing Up

Being a C_3 African American does not make a person sell-out nor unsympathetic to institutional racism. It simply means the individual is working for justice by using influence *within the dominant culture*, rather than from the outside.

A C_2 Black person is bi-cultural. Her culture is split down the center between the prevailing culture and inner-city culture. This means she has some elements of the dominant culture and some elements of urban culture. For example, Sandra lives in a predominantly Black urban neighborhood, but goes to work in the prevailing White world, and was educated at institutions formed by the dominant culture. She lives in the hood, but works in an upscale office downtown, and graduated from high school with honors.

During any given day, she adapts to the environment in which she finds herself. Her actions, thinking, speech, and body language change according to the culture around her. She dresses one way at work and another way at home; her speech changes according to her audience, making her able to fit into both cultures.

A C_1 African American lives, works, and was educated in the inner city. His thinking, education, and cultural preferences are adapted to survival in the inner city. De'Andre works at the neighborhood store and was educated to survive on the streets, thriving within a completely different set of rules for behavior from the prevailing C_3 culture. What he considers important and beautiful, how he exchanges information, and how he relates to others in his community are dramatically different from C_3 people, even those sharing his skin color. Both his vocation and education would be viewed as less than ideal by the prevailing culture.

Hispanic Examples

Maria is a Latina who lives in a middle-class neighborhood, works as an accountant, and graduated with a college degree. Her grandparents immigrated to the U.S. from Latin America, but she does not speak Spanish. Maria is C_3 despite her ethnicity.

Carlos lives, works, and was educated in a combination of dominant culture and city culture and so is "C_2" (a bi-cultural person). He lives in a low-income area, but works as a clerk at City Hall, having studied for a year at community college. Carlos speaks English at work and Spanish in his neighborhood. He understands the culture of the inner city but also knows how to survive in the prevailing culture, switching back and forth between two worlds throughout the day, thriving in each one.

By contrast, his uncle Hector, who lives next door to Carlos, works as a janitor at the neighborhood school. He quit school to get a job and speaks very little English. Hector would be comfortable in C_1 Hispanic culture.

Also, keep in mind that not all Hispanics are culturally the same. Immigrants from Guatemala are different than those from Mexico or Paraguay. Just because they speak the same language does not mean they have the same cultural preferences, or that they even get along with each other.

Anglo Examples

Betty lives in a gated community, works as an attorney, and got a graduate degree from a local university, making her C_3.

Climbing Up

Sherry lives in a Section 8 apartment building among mostly White people. She takes the bus to work where she is a medical receptionist, after completing two years of college. Sherry is an example of C_2.

Bill lives in trailer park among other working-class poor Anglos. He finished high school but never did well in school. He enjoys his construction job and serves in his local church. Bill is an example of a C_1 White person.

Asian Examples

Stanley (C_3) is an investment banker who lives in an upscale area and graduated from a prestigious university. His grandparents (C_1) were refugees from Laos, started a restaurant in a low-income area, and never learned English. They lived in an apartment above the restaurant until recently, when Stanley purchased a home for his parents and grandparents to live in together. Stanley's father (C_2) is bilingual and continues to run the restaurant in the old neighborhood.

Like the other examples, not all Asian cultures are the same, especially since they speak different languages and have vastly different preferences. These examples serve as general descriptions for the purpose of demonstrating the complexities of cultural differences.

Not a Value Judgment

None of these descriptions are meant to make a value judgment, but to describe the sub-cultural differences in American cities. The differences in C_1, C_2, and C_3 are profound and they can generate much disagreement, even within the same ethnic group.

For example, one of our friends grew up in a Black family where his father served in the Armed Forces. He did not grow up in the hood, although many of his cousins did. He is an executive of a prison ministry. His bi-cultural perspective gives him the ability to relate to either the Black or White community, giving him a different perspective on ethnic relations than many of his C_1 prison students.

Don is another C_2 example. He was educated in the dominant culture, having earned a graduate degree, and lived in a mixed (but predominantly White) neighborhood. But for 30 years he *worked* in inner city Los Angeles among the urban poor. This experience gave him the ability to bridge both C_1 and C_3 cultures as a C_2 Anglo.

<u>Implications for Ministry</u>

These observations about culture guided World Impact into more effective ministry in the city. For example, it finally made sense why a new C_1 convert would feel uncomfortable at a C_3 church. While their skin color might be the same, the manner of dress, decorum, and financial practices were different, and those contrasts came through loud and clear during the worship service.

This is best understood in historic context. In the 60s and 70s, many African American churches were attended by educated, professional people who moved out of the neighborhood when housing laws changed. The members no longer lived in the church's inner-city area, but commuted in from other areas each Sunday. These churches had become C_3 churches based on the economic and educational levels of the congregants. As a result, C_1 converts living nearby would feel out of place, and in order to fit in, they would feel the need to change cultures from C_1 to C_3 (or stop attending altogether). The net result was virtually no culturally-comfortable C_1 churches, led by C_1 leaders in the inner-city.

Climbing Up

These realities led World Impact to understand C_1 culture as an unreached people group, and the American inner city as an unreached mission field. There was a need to plant new churches in this mission field, where C_3 missionaries could empower C_1 Christians to lead churches in their own C_1 cultural context. In other words, a C_1 believer did not have to change cultures to be legitimate and feel at home in church.

A Precedent in Church History

Fortunately, there was a precedent in Acts 15 for this kind of cultural dynamic in Church history. As shown in the diagram below, when the Gentiles first came to faith, there was pressure for them to change culture and become Jewish to be followers of Christ.

Biblical Precedence (Acts 15)

Gentile ⟶ Jew ⟶ Follower of Christ

But at this turning point in history, Gentiles could be fully accepted as followers of Christ without having to become culturally Jewish.

Gentile ⟶ ~~Jew~~ ⟶ Follower of Christ

In the same way, at first a C_1 Black believer was expected to adapt to a C_3 Black church to be a follower of Christ.

C_1 ⟶ C_3 ⟶ Follower of Christ

But having a clearer understanding about what was happening, a C_1 believer could be a legitimate follower of Jesus without changing culture. They could retain their C_1 cultural preferences and still be a full member in the Body of Christ. In fact, a C_1 person could even be a leader in a C_1 church without changing into the framework of the dominant culture.[3]

$$C_1 \longrightarrow \cancel{C_3} \longrightarrow \textbf{Follower of Christ}$$

Conclusion

These lessons from Church history, and the dynamics of culture in American cities, are examples to help you see the hidden complexities of prison and civilian culture. The rhythm of life in prison is different from the rhythm of the free world, because of cultural differences. Charles Anderson told us, "For our men coming out of prison, understanding these different rhythms is where we gain or lose them in re-entry."

Every culture is full of complexity, so you need to learn how to recognize cultural differences as you are Climbing Up.

Questions for Reflection

1. Study the American sub-culture diagram. Based on where you lived, worked, and were educated, where do you fit and why?

2. Using the diagram, pick out two people with whom you can talk about this subject and ask them what they think about their own cultural background.

3. Read Acts 15. What do you observe about cultural differences among the people of God that might relate to your prison and re-entry experience?

Chapter 3
Elements of Prison Culture

CULTURE IS THE SET of rules and behaviors that someone must follow to enjoy a decent life. To have a good life in Canada, you follow Canadian expectations of behavior. To have good life in China, you follow Chinese expectations of behavior. To have good life in a jungle of Peru, you follow the expectations of that village.

Prison is the same way. You had to learn these rules and conform with them to survive. Acclimation to culture is not a bad thing, it simply means you have successfully adjusted to your environment.

According to Prison Fellowship, a person is fully enculturated into prison culture after 18-24 months of exposure (and sometimes sooner).[4] Therefore, regardless of your background, you will adapt to the culture of prison within the first two years. Whether you actually committed a crime or were falsely arrested, after 24 months of incarceration, you were enculturated into prison culture, or what we call "C_p."

This means that no matter what you did before (doctor, lawyer, drug dealer, pastor, or construction worker), if you have survived your time in prison, your behavior has changed. You have enculturated. And the longer you have been in prison, the more normal C_p culture has become.

The following eight elements of C_p culture are a sample among others that could be mentioned.

Climbing Up

Decision Making

One of the most powerful expressions of prison enculturation is the restriction of choices. Quentin Valdois told us, "Everything is designed to repress your sense of individuality, independence, and autonomy and to replace it with herd mentality, dependence, and subjection. Eventually, to function in this new culture, you accept this reality, play your part, and over time this becomes normal."

You may have observed how prison robs people of opportunities for independent thinking. As freedoms are restricted and choices become limited, decision-making muscles can atrophy. There is no choice about what to wear, what to eat, or when to eat. Prisoners cannot choose where to live. They must go where they are told, at the time they are told, and be instructed to report to one location only to be suddenly sent to another place (without advance warning).

These high levels of control naturally affect a prisoner's ability to make decisions and take proactive responsibility. When choices about food, clothing, housing, are forced upon them, it can generate a sense of entitlement ("You owe me"). If a person is not careful, it can lead into victimization ("Oh well, there's nothing I can do"). Both entitlement and victimization result in reduced capacity to make decisions which makes it difficult to function in civilian culture, where the number of daily choices abound.

Constant Vigilance

Another element of C_p culture is the need for constant vigilance. As you know, the environment of prison is dangerous, so inmates must be constantly aware of imminent attack. Prisoners can be beaten or humiliated by guards or other prisoners without provocation. This exposure to violence and abuse, without the ability to stop it or ignore it, creates a natural suspicion of everyone. It also influences how prisoners relate to the events around them.

Personal Space

One way this can be understood is the matter of personal space. Anyone who gets too close will be viewed as a threat. For example, Alan was in a clothing store shortly after release, feeling anxious that another shopper was too close to him. He said he had the urge to turn around and hit the shopper in the face for being so close.

Sudden Movement

In prison, the formation of large crowds or sudden movement is a sign of trouble. Gary said he was on the yard playing cards when the person next to him was murdered. He knew if he jumped up and ran away it would arouse the guards into thinking a riot was forming, and he might be shot. To avoid injury, he and his friends sat next to the corpse for several minutes until they could slowly get up and walk away.

Church Services

The structure of a worship service in prison is different than the outside. Prisoners are dismissed one row at a time to thank the preacher. But on the outside people get up and down all through the service, and at the conclusion everyone exits randomly, in several different directions.

Sheila said the first time she went to church on the outside, she was so frightened by the people leaving in such a chaotic way that she ran to hide behind a door until everyone left the building. She was also disturbed that the people did not go up to greet the preacher at the conclusion of the service.

Climbing Up

Other Behaviors

There are behaviors that seem unusual to people in free-world culture. For example, in prison it is normal for you to listen to another person while constantly glancing around the room to assess potential threats. But on the outside, such behavior would imply you were not paying full attention to the other person.

Also, the fear of imminent danger in prison causes some prisoners to sleep without covers so they can escape quickly from a threatening situation. When this persists in the free world, family members find this to be puzzling.

Signs of Disrespect

In C_p culture, respect is highly valued. Think about what you see in your prison and you will notice expressions of disrespect like snitching, asking personal questions, cutting in line, sitting in someone else's assigned seat, being in debt to someone, or not keeping a promise.

Don was mentoring Jeff, who asked Don's advice on how to deal with a grant writer who volunteered to help Jeff raise money for his new ministry. After several weeks, the volunteer had not responded, and Jeff did not know what to do. Don told Jeff to email the volunteer and say, "You may have become too busy to help me set up my ministry and if so, that is ok. But I'd like to find someone else to help if you are not able." Jeff was stunned, and after a long pause, he said, "I never would have thought of that. In prison, I would simply go confront the person for disrespecting me and not keeping his word."

Respect is so important in prison culture that it affects one's use of humor. What is understood as good-natured ribbing in civilian life can be taken as a serious sign of disrespect in prison. On the outside, returning citizens might be viewed as cold, threatening, and overly serious simply because they misinterpret harmless remarks as threats to be challenged.

Showing Strength

If you study what happens in your prison, you will see that C_p culture values strength, especially in men's prisons, where the strong prey upon the weak. A prisoner must appear strong or be at risk for attack. Therefore, it is important for prisoners to mask their feelings to seem tough. Demonstrating strength may also include standing in harm's way as a sign of loyalty to the group.[5] Prompt retaliation is often required to demonstrate strength, which creates a culture of quick response ("handling your business").

It is counter to prison culture to calm down before acting because it indicates weakness. If someone disrespects you, it is mandatory that you handle it immediately. This produces a culture where people act before thinking it through, which runs counter to acceptable problem-solving and conflict resolution skills in free-world culture.

View of Reality

If your prison is confined to a small geographical area and a limited population, it can function like a small-town, with a provincial attitude that distorts reality.

In civilian culture, people often appreciate the exchange of a broad range of diverse ideas and non-defensive dialogue. However, C_p culture is organized around tightly held personal opinions or tribal allegiances (e.g. gangs or other sub-groups). Such resistance to free and open debate creates the potential for closed-mindedness and extreme defensiveness. So the smallest challenge in thinking can be interpreted as a major offense, even leading to violence. Arguments can break out over insignificant disagreements.

Self-Justification

In such an environment, self-justification can set in, where prisoners listen only to those who agree with them. This aspect of C_p culture produces a warped view of reality. Rather than admitting their faults, they may habitually defend themselves and blame others. Such belief can grow into victimization, where people say things like, "The system is out to get me."

Entitlement

A related distortion is a sense of entitlement, a belief that "I should get whatever I want, whenever I want it." Those who are affected by this C_p notion will become confused about the difference between rights and responsibilities, between wants and needs. This can be recognized when they either 1) emphasize their rights (but feel little sense of responsibility); or 2) believe anything they want is something they must have. And when either of these unrealistic expectations goes unfulfilled, their entire self-image can feel threatened, leading to an explosion of rage.[6]

Unique Thinking

You may have observed a more extreme form of distorted C_p reality called "unique thinking."[7] This is where people believe they are superior to others, existing in a class by themselves. This assumption produces pride, overconfidence, or a reckless regard for the well-being of others, where remorse, humility, and repentance are rare. "Unique thinking" can become so blinding that the person might even say, "If I think it, it must be so."

Idealistic

Distorted reality can emerge when someone has too much time on their hands. Eager for time to pass, people immerse themselves into idealistic dreams about their former life that no longer exits. They remember their old neighborhood in a way that has long since passed or imagine family members as they were but have since grown old during their incarceration. Longing for the days when they once felt invincible, they forget the bad days, creating a false memory of the past. Entertaining fantasies about the way things were sets them up for grief and disappointment when reality sets in upon release.

Constant Interaction

Think about your prison and notice what a highly social environment it is, where human interaction is constant. It can be shocking for former prisoners to see people so disconnected from one another on the outside. Christians accustomed to continual fellowship with their brothers (or sisters) all day, are often surprised to find Christians in the free world gathering only one or two times a week. The difference in social intensity can lead former prisoners to view those on the outside as lukewarm or lacking in commitment.

Prisons are also loud and intense. There is persistent noise and annoying conversations that cannot be avoided. Prisoners and prison officials tend to speak at higher volume than those in the free world. When prisoners get out, if they are loud, direct, and intense, they will seem scary and socially awkward to people on the outside. Returning citizens must learn to "take the volume down a notch" (or two or three). Also, a healthy theological dialogue among brothers or sisters in prison would be viewed as a divisive and frightening shouting match in civilian culture.

Climbing Up

In women's prisons, even though they are surrounded by people, prisoners often have intense feelings of isolation and loneliness. This is because they tend to get less emotional support from their families than male prisoners. They feel the loss of connection with their children in different ways than men. Women compensate with this loss by seeking strong relational connections with other prisoners, while male prisoners cope by appearing tough and emotionally distant.

Bartering Economy

You may have noticed that the economy of prison is based on bartering and trading services. Successful prisoners develop the ability to "hustle," an assertive behavior to get something for nothing, to take advantage of a situation. Prisoners learn to ask favors from everyone they can, even when they are able to do something for themselves. In most cases, this is the natural way of commerce in C_p. In the worst case, the process of exchange can be used to manipulate or intimidate others, just for the thrill of it.

In civilian life, people will be offended by this way of doing business, puzzled by the persistent request for favors. Others may think, "Why can't he do that for himself?" and misjudge the former prisoner to be a lazy person, rather than recognizing this as a cultural difference.

At the same time, you should check your own motives, being aware of using excess praise, flattery, or confiding in others as a form of manipulation. Ask the Lord to show you when you are using a person for what they can give, rather than valuing them as a person.

Persistent Loss

Look at the physical surroundings of your prison. It is probably is a life-draining physical environment of concrete, steel, and drab colors. If you have signs of life such as animals, trees, grass, or bright colors, your situation is unusual. But even the best environment cannot mask another element of C_p culture: the persistent sense of shame, disappointment, and loss.

Losses are felt every day: loss of freedom, loss of money, loss of beautiful surroundings, loss of friends who may be transferred to another prison, loss of privacy, loss of dignity through public showers and toilets, loss of access to loved ones. The constant monotony of the daily grind can lead prisoners into escapism, pursuing all kinds of distractions to fill the day.

Because of this ever-present sense of loss, discouragement, and hopelessness, any celebration of positive events or accomplishments may be met with resentment or ridicule.[8] And when celebrations do occur, they can be cancelled at the last minute. We participated in a graduation ceremony that was scheduled for 90 minutes. Shortly after the ceremony began, there was a lockdown in the facility, and we had only 15 more minutes to compress the ceremony before being hurried out the gate.

Another source of loss is the short amount of time available for meals. Sometimes lockdowns or delays can even eliminate a meal. We took Bennie to dinner at a restaurant shortly after release. After studying the menu for a long time, he asked for help, explaining that the choices were too overwhelming. After a few minutes, he stopped our conversation and said, "I am having a hard time adjusting to a leisurely dinner when in prison we had to hurry up and eat. There was no time for talking like this."

Persistent loss is also caused by the lack of privacy in small living spaces. Prisoners are constantly subject to search, all mail is reviewed, and phone calls are recorded. Living in a confined area affects how prisoners act. For example, some learn to sleep with arms extended across at their sides so they do not roll out of bed and fall to the floor, a habit that may continue into civilian life.

Conclusion

Decision making, constant vigilance, signs of disrespect, showing strength, distorted reality, constant interaction, bartering economy, and persistent loss are eight elements of prison culture, C_p. The more you observe the culture you are in, the better you can adjust to life on the outside.

Next, we turn our attention to how C_p culture clashes with free-world culture.

Questions for Reflection

1. For each of the eight examples of prison culture (C_p), write down an example where you have seen this at work.

2. Make a list of other elements of prison culture that are not listed in the eight examples.

3. Using the list of eight examples, and your list from #2, select three elements and describe how each one will be challenging in your transition to civilian culture.

Chapter 4
Clashes with Civilian Culture

IT IS ONE THING to recognize acceptable patterns of behavior while incarcerated, but it takes a new skill to acclimate to civilian culture. Chet said, "You can put me in any state prison in America, and I know how to get along. I know what to do. But when I got out on the streets, I had no idea what to do." Had Chet understood what to expect, he would have been better equipped to make the cultural shift upon his release. The following six warnings, each ending with an "antidote," will help you as your are Climbing Up.

Appearing Unapproachable

Because you are accustomed to a C_p environment of constant danger, when you get out you will continue to be vigilant, assessing the danger around you. This culture of suspicion can make it difficult to transition to civilian life where people relate to one another in a more relaxed, open, and vulnerable way. For example, you may leave crowded situations abruptly, before conversations have naturally ended. Or you may stand too far away from a group, giving the sense that you are unfriendly or not interested in talking with them.

In prison, vulnerability and transparency are viewed as weakness. Trusting people, including those in authority, leaves prisoners susceptible to injury. By contrast, on the outside, those who seem warm and trusting have an easier time building healthy relationships and networks. Because of this cultural clash, your lack of trust can make you appear cold and private, resulting in difficulty forming friendships.

This can extend to the dynamics of worship services. While the rest of the church finds it natural to get up from their seat to get coffee or greet someone across the room, because of your prison worship experience, you might feel glued to your seat. As a result, you may seem tense or unapproachable.

Finally, because prisoners are deprived of decisions related to fashion, they are unable to express themselves through the clothes they wear. For this reason tattoos can serve as a symbol of personal expression. However, tattoos can be shocking to those in civilian culture because they are often associated with criminal behavior, especially to older adults.

The antidote for "Appearing Unapproachable" is to be teachable and have a sense of humor. Ask friends to tell you how you are being perceived and when you do things that seem strange. Be willing to laugh at yourself when you make cultural mistakes. It will get better.

Unwarranted Fears

Because of your experiences in prison, you may assume there is danger where none exists. For example, Karl told about his need to ride the bus to get to the social security office. When the bus pulled up, it was jammed with people. The image of an unknown crowd packed together triggered a sense of panic and he was unable to board. Instead, he walked six hours to and from the office in order to avoid the crowded bus. He barely got back to his re-entry home before being locked out at curfew.

Many fears in free-world culture can be associated with the number of decisions to be made every day. You probably know how to navigate the rigid structure of prisons. You know where to go and not to go and you have adjusted to the routine. Upon release, the freedom can be overwhelming, like being dropped into a foreign country.

For example, when Fred was released, his friends took him straight to Starbucks to get coffee. Stunned by the dozens of options and combinations, Fred was paralyzed to make a decision. When it became his turn to order, he felt embarrassed and stammered, "Do you guys sell coffee here?"

The antidote for "Unwarranted Fears" is to be humble enough to talk to civilian friends about your experiences. Do not expect them to see what you see. Had Karl told a friend he was afraid to get on a crowded bus, his friend could have arranged a short ride together to preview a longer bus trip. When faced with a new situation, like at Starbucks, it is perfectly appropriate to tell the cashier, "This is my first time here, so please help me figure out what to order."

New-found Freedom

Mark Walker explains a "honeymoon period" when a former prisoner is first released and experiences everything in a fresh way. It can feel like a new-birth experience. But shortly after release, disappointment will come if your expectations are too high. If you do not learn how to do spiritual warfare while incarcerated, when you face setback, you can fall quickly.

The sheer number of decisions and choices to be made each day can be completely overwhelming, such as what products to buy, which way to get to work, or how to spend your free time.

Being released from C_p level of control, where you are told what you eat, wear and how you spend your time, can be a source of joy but also a source of anxiety and temptation. While you have been incarcerated, new ways to access sinful behavior have been created through technology, and you <u>will</u> be vulnerable. Many former prisoners believed they were immune from the enemy's attempts to destroy them and were caught by surprise.

They did not develop a healthy respect for the deception of evil, and when temptation came, they either doubted their salvation or fell back into old patterns of substance abuse. Some even encountered freedom like a college freshman who gets away from the rules of home and goes crazy partying.

But substance abuse is not the only way the enemy can distract you. Consumerism is another pitfall you can face. Zeb told us that one of the activities he loved to do upon release was to walk through Wal Mart and marvel at the wide variety of products available. After years of the limitations of the prison store, Zeb would return from shopping to discover he had purchased far more products than he could afford.

The antidote to "New-found Freedom" is to prepare yourself in three ways:

1. While in prison, practice daily decision-making exercises to prevent those muscles from atrophying. Make plans for your release including action steps to find a job, church, housing, and transportation. Formulate a schedule for your daily routine and how you will discipline yourself regarding time stewardship among competing demands for family, job search, and church fellowship. Revisit and revise these plans periodically

2. Learn to resist temptation while incarcerated, fully expecting the devil to continue to tempt you on the outside, probably with even greater intensity. Take the opportunity God has given you to address your spiritual and emotional problems now, because you will not have as much time to do so when you get out. Make

every effort to take any pre-release courses that are offered. Classes using interactive journaling are particularly helpful, especially from *The Change Companies®*.

3. Take advantage of every educational or vocational opportunity that is offered during your incarceration. It is unlikely you will find a paying job in ministry when you get out, but even if you do, God will use every class you take in your future service to Him. Use the time to broaden yourself in every possible way, because you do not know what skill God might use down the road. Adding tools to your toolbelt will create additional opportunities in civilian culture.

Big Begets Big

In the world, big begets big, but in the Kingdom of God, *small begets big*. Jesus illustrates this principle in the parables of the leaven and mustard seed (Mt. 13:31-33). It is the slow and steady growth that produces lasting value. Watch out for fantastic schemes that smell like "big begets big." For example, Ricardo told us that he imagined himself being released and starting a worldwide television ministry, only to find that his dream was dashed when no one would listen to him, even at his home church. He eventually gave up and stopped going to church altogether.

If Ricardo had used the slow and steady approach that bears fruit over the long haul, he could have seen his teaching gift grow steadily over time. For example, he could have attended a Bible study where he built relationships, encouraged people from the Word, and prayed for them. As they slowly got to know him, observing his love for the Scriptures, they would recognize his teaching gift and ask for his opinion. Then, out of this growing respect, opportunities for teaching would naturally occur.

Climbing Up

The antidote for "Big Begets Big" is to start small and be faithful. Grow your vision one step at a time.

Differences in Christian Community

Another potential clash in culture relates to Christian community. Many prisoners are accustomed to having Christian friends around to study the Bible, encourage each other, and share the gospel. They have a brotherhood (or sisterhood) that is similar to those who went through a war together. Like veterans, you will return to a civilian life that does not understand what you have been through, and you may be disappointed to find that the church on the outside is not like the C_p brotherhood you had in prison.

Another difference is related to time. In prison, there is ample time for fellowship and study. In fact, time is an enemy in prison because there is *too much* time available; it does not move quickly enough. Prisoners often wish time would go by faster so they can be released or escape boredom. In civilian culture, time is an enemy because there is *not enough* available (time moves too quickly). American life is hectic and people always seem busy.

You may also experience pronounced racial segregation in free-world churches. While most prisons are highly segregated, with prisoners associating among racially divided gangs, Christians who refuse to participate in gangs often become friends with believers from all the other ethnic groups in prison. This creates a Christian fellowship that is highly integrated. If this is your C_p experience, you may find it uncomfortable to be among Christian friends who represent a single ethnic group.

The other major adjustment is the presence of the opposite sex and children. Prisoners are accustomed to living with only men or only women. Coming to a church with members of both sexes can be awkward at first.

Do not Give Up

In your effort to adjust to these differences in Christian community, you may be tempted to pull back from church altogether. But it is essential to find Christian friends right away because they are the best ones to help you navigate the new culture. If you do not seek out Christian friends to help you acclimate in a Christlike way, you will probably go back to your old criminal friends who are more accessible. Research and experience show that doing so will lead you back to prison.[9] Remember, bad company corrupts good character (1 Cor. 15:33).

Christian friends help you shift from C_p influences, gain a different perspective, and overcome temptations at a time when your defenses are down. Having godly friends will motivate you to resist risky and self-defeating behavior. You need Christian friends more than you need a job, more than you need housing, more than you need transportation. They will help you make the cultural transition to succeed in civilian culture.

The antidote for "Differences in Christian Community" is to find Christian friends immediately and stay committed to them even when it is difficult.

Making Up for Lost Time

Arguably, the most dangerous mistake that former prisoners make in their re-entry is the desperate attempt to *make up for lost time*. When you are released, you may feel extreme pressure within yourself (or from family members) to hurry up and redeem the time you lost in prison. There is an urgency to spend all your time with family (to make up for lost family time); all your time making money (to make up for lost income); all your time doing ministry (to pay back for the destruction you caused to society). You may want to quickly get married to avoid sexual temptation and make up for lost time sexually.

Instead of a mad rush to open a business, start a new ministry, or reconnect with family and friends all at once, it is far better to spread out your activities over the long term. Do not take on too much at first. Prov. 28:20 says, "A faithful man will be richly blessed, but one eager to get rich will not go unpunished." Success comes by being faithful over the long haul and not by quick accomplishments.

The parable of the talents reminds us of this truth: "*After a long time* the master of those servants returned and settled accounts with them. The man who had received five bags of gold brought the other five. 'Master,' he said, 'you entrusted me with five bags of gold. See, I have gained five more.' His master replied, 'Well done, good and faithful servant! You have been faithful with a few things; I will put you in charge of many things. Come and share your master's happiness!'" (Mt. 25:19, *emphasis added*).

Climbing Up takes time, and it cannot be done in one short burst of manic activity. In fact, it is our strong belief, and the opinion of many others, that it will take 12-18 months of sustained effort in Christian community to shift from prison to civilian culture.[10] Although getting a job, restoring family relationships, and serving in a local church will help you in your journey, it will not shorten the time it takes to mentally adjust to the new culture.

Just like missionaries who move overseas and adjust to a new culture, you must be patient and go through the process over at least 12-18 months. But you can do it, especially when you are aware of the process!

The antidote for "Making Up for Lost Time" is to go slow and be faithful in little before being faithful in much. Go slow!

Conclusion

Appearing unapproachable, unwarranted fears, new-found freedom, big begets big, differences in Christian community, and making up for lost time are six potential clashes between your C_p experience and life on the outside. As you are Climbing Up, you will need to be ready to face them with courage and patience.

Questions for Reflection

1. For each of the six potential clashes with culture, describe how you felt when you read about each one. Were you surprised by any of them? Did you want to argue that they were not true in your experience?

2. What other clashes with culture might you expect that were not listed in this chapter?

3. For each of the six potential clashes, describe in detail how you plan to handle each one upon release.

Chapter 5
Unspoken Assumptions

NOW THAT YOU HAVE reviewed how you have been shaped by C_p culture it will be helpful to understand some of the pre-conceptions that civilians have about returning citizens.

Source of Conflicts

In our personal life-experience, we have generally found that the primary source of conflicts come from unspoken assumptions we make about a situation. You assume one thing, your co-worker assumes something else, and then conflict erupts when each person's expectations are not met. The solution is to bring our thoughts out into the open.

As you consider life on the outside, be aware that you have assumptions that are probably different than what your family, friends, and society are thinking. Conversely, they may be surprised to discover that prisoners have their own fears about being released from prison. This leaves a situation where everyone harbors unspoken assumptions, without the chance for dialogue leading to mutual understanding. But when such expectations are brought into the open, it will minimize unnecessary disappointment and hurt feelings.

Civilian Perceptions

People have a wide variety of opinions about prisoners being released into their community. Some may be eager to welcome you, while others wish you would have never been released.

Climbing Up

Prejudices

Some will have prejudices about you because they do not know a prisoner and have never visited a prison. This kind of person has formed opinions by watching television or movies and does not have an accurate picture of what prison is really like. They may be gripped with fear when thinking about relating to someone who has been incarcerated. So if you meet someone like this for the first time, remember they are reacting to an image they have from media, not to you as a person. Do not take their reaction personally.

Uncertainty

Others may be highly motivated to welcome former prisoners to their church, but at the same time feel anxiety about what that might mean. While they have heard of miraculous transformation, they have also heard stories of self-proclaimed Christians committing terrible crimes upon their release. They may be anxious about their welfare and the safety of others in the church, especially the children.

There may also be apprehension that former prisoners are wolves in sheep's clothing who will prey upon good-hearted and naïve servants in the church. They may even imagine prisoners dropped off at the church door in busloads, rather than each person quietly joining the community one by one. This notion can lead to fear that that returning citizens will bring an unsavory element to the community, where the church is over-run by former prisoners, so they no longer feel at home in their own church. Or they fear that potential new members may be scared away by this threatening atmosphere.

Resentment

Some people may be the victims of crime and find it difficult to forgive those who damaged their lives or their loved ones. The last thing they want is to have former prisoners in their church, a constant reminder of their loss. Or they may be embarrassed to reveal that their own sons, husbands, nieces, uncles, or friends are incarcerated. Welcoming a former prisoner might open a door they prefer to keep shut.

Burdensome

There also may be concern about the burden placed on the church. They fear that welcoming former prisoners, their wives, and children may sap the church's strength so that it is no longer able to care for everyone in the congregation. They may assume they must start a half-way house or hire more staff with specialized expertise. It may be overwhelming to add what they see as yet another program to the church when they can barely keep up with what they are already doing.

Failure

Another fear civilians have is failure. They do not want to start welcoming former prisoners, fail, then give up in embarrassment. It may be easier to never start down this road than to be forced to turn back in disgrace.

None of these assumptions relate to you as an individual, but they are real fears that people have about prisoners in general. They will rarely be said out loud but need to be understood as invisible assumptions of civilian culture.

Despite the apprehensions that churches have about the formerly incarcerated, there are many who are eager to step out in faith, give you a chance, and come alongside you to ensure your success. They will pray for you, believe in you, and help you navigate the new environment of civilian culture. Some will already have experience in helping former prisoners, and others will be new to the process. But the responsibility is yours to prepare yourself now on the inside, so you can love these brothers and sisters in Christ as they partner with your re-entry.

Moving Along a Continuum

This may be difficult to hear but it is true: there is a stigma attached to those coming out of prison. But despite this stigma, God can help people change their thinking about returning citizens, and it often happens in steps, moving along a continuum.

Pathological

At one end of the continuum, many people view prisoners as pathetic and pathological, with no hope of redemption. They believe it is wasteful to invest time or energy on prisoners who will never be useful.

Pity

As people become more educated, they may move along the spectrum from viewing prisoners as "pathological," to being moved by "pity." Out of the compassion in their hearts they start to feel badly for prisoners' plight and want to help. However, they view prisoners as pitiful and needy, and may even make offensive references to prisoners, such as "modern-day lepers."

Patronizing

As others come to know a prisoner personally, they may move from "pity" to "patronizing." They begin to see that prisoners have something to offer, but only with "my help." In other words, they do not believe that prisoners will ever function at "my level," and what limited potential is there will require significant and on-going assistance from the patron.

Partnership

God moves some along the continuum from "patronizing" to "partnership." They start to understand the truth of Js. 2:5: "God has chosen the poor to be rich in faith and inherit the Kingdom." When their eyes are opened to the true capacity of the incarcerated, they become even more motivated to invest their energy. They begin to think, "Prisoners can surpass me with just a little bit of my effort." In these cases, prisoners become friends and co-laborers, producing a return that is 30, 60, or 100 times the mentor's investment.

Wherever a civilian might be on this continuum, give them grace in their journey. Follow Paul's instructions in Eph. 4:1-3 "I therefore, a prisoner for the Lord, urge you to walk in a manner worthy of the calling to which you have been called, with all humility and gentleness, with patience, bearing with one another in love, eager to maintain the unity of the Spirit in the bond of peace." God was patient with you, so extend that patience to others.

You cannot stop others from judging you; you must accept it. But you do not have to let others define you. God knows you perfectly and accepts you fully. Others might reject you without getting to know you. But live into the truth of what *God says,* not what others think. Take responsibility for your own actions and leave them to work out their prejudices with the Lord.

Climbing Up

Awkward Surprises

Some unspoken assumptions can result in awkward surprises. One of these relates to housing. You may assume that you are moving back home upon release. But just because your family has visited you in prison does not mean they are prepared to have you move in with them. Some families wait until the last minute to inform the returning citizen they are not welcomed back, leaving the released prisoner homeless with nowhere to go.

Or you might be welcomed home only to find a difficult adjustment because your family has learned how to function without you. Therefore, it is important to clarify everyone's expectations well in advance of your release.

Also, you may be surprised by friends who relate to you in offensive ways. For example, in their effort to help you re-build your decision-making muscles, they may refuse to help you make a decision. Or they may go in the other direction and treat you like a child, forcing you to live under strict rules and regulations.

Another kind of surprise comes when people in the church respond in odd ways about money. They may have heard that the economy of prison culture creates master manipulators, so they assume you are taking advantage of people at every opportunity. They may be wary of enabling you, afraid of being swindled, or being perceived as an easy mark.

Because of this dynamic, we suggest that you do not ask anyone (except immediate family) about moving into their home. It is better to wait for them to offer. Build a trust relationship with people before asking for too many favors.

<u>Facing Your Fears</u>

In the months leading up to your release, you can prepare yourself for life on the outside by articulating your own fears related to civilian culture. Keeping your fears bottled up will not help you take aggressive action to overcome them. For example, many returning citizens report that when they get out, they feel like everyone can tell that they have been in prison, as though they have a sign on their back saying, "formerly incarcerated."

You may feel this way as you adjust to a new culture, but that does not mean anyone notices your struggle. This self-conscious feeling is normal and will subside over time. In the meantime, try to relax. If someone stares at you, it does not mean they think you have just been released from prison.

Also, remember that people are not conspiring against you, even though it can feel that way at times. Mary Flin, who develops Christian leaders inside and outside prison, said, "Everybody doesn't hate you, but not everybody is going to be nice to you. You have to be OK with the fact that not everyone cares if you succeed. Yet, not everyone is against you either. Some people are just having their own bad days."

Disrespect

You may be a trained minister or a recognized leader in the church inside prison. Therefore, you may wonder if you will receive the same level of respect and acceptance on the outside. You may fear that no matter what you do, you will never escape the consequences of your incarceration. Even though you feel God's forgiveness, you worry that you will never receive acceptance by other Christians.

Climbing Up

Finding Community

You may have received Christ in prison and do not even know how to look for a church on the outside. You have experienced an amazing brotherhood or sisterhood inside prison, where you live in community 24/7, under the most extreme adversity. Perhaps you have been persecuted for your faith, to the point that if you did not live up to your testimony, you were in physical danger.

In such a violent community where you cannot escape, you enjoy a constant source of strength from other believers. You fear that upon release you will not find that same level of support and be forced to live out your faith alone. You hope you can find a church to use your gifts but fear you will never have the same level of comradery you enjoyed inside prison.

Employment

You may also fear that upon release, you might not find a job and become unable to provide for yourself or your family. This can be especially distressing if you feel that you disappointed your family while in prison. Or you may feel a debt to family members who sacrificed for many years and say, "Now it's my turn to care for you."

Changes in Society

The fear of stepping into a rapidly changing society, especially related to technology, is quite common. You may not know how to use the internet or cell phones. Your old neighborhood may have changed dramatically. You fear temptations you have never faced before that could overwhelm you. You do not want to forsake the Lord and go back to your old ways. Apprehensive about being alone or rejected, you may be concerned that you will end up back to prison.

If you are experiencing any of these fears, bring them out into the open so God can help you think about them in light of His truth. Look through the Bible (or ask Christian friends) for verses to meditate on that address your fears, trusting the Spirit to give you hope. In Part II, we will provide a practical exercise to help you overcome your fears and replace them with confidence.

Conclusion

Unspoken assumptions are a primary source of disappointment and interpersonal conflict. Civilians have pre-conceived notions, fears, and hopes. So do you. Bringing them into the light is a good way to begin Climbing Up.

Questions for Reflection

1. In addition to the fear civilians have about prisoners, what other feelings might people have about you joining their community?

2. In addition to the list of fears prisoners have in this chapter, what other apprehensions do you have about acclimating to civilian culture?

3. Make a plan to pro-actively address these fears, using Scripture as much as you can.

Chapter 6
The Process of Re-enculturation

NOW THAT YOU HAVE been introduced to some of the cultural differences, and the fears associated with the process of re-entry, it is time to consider proactive steps you can take toward re-enculturation.

If you have a group of Christian friends waiting to receive you, people who have educated themselves in differences between civilian and C_p culture, you are in the best position to re-enculturate because they will help you navigate the process.

If your Christian friends on the outside are not educated on the cultural differences, you should encourage them to read this book, or go through *The Onesimus Workshop* video we produced, available at Amazon.com. If they learn the dynamics you will be facing, it will be a significant service to you (and others in their Christian community).

If you do not have a people waiting for you, it will be a more difficult process to re-enculturate, but you can do it! You will need to take personal responsibility, find a group of Christian friends, and persevere when it gets difficult. <u>One thing is sure, you cannot make the cultural shift alone; relationships are key.</u> The following prescriptions will help you acclimate to civilian culture.

Take Personal Responsibility

One of the damaging effects of prison culture is self-justification and blaming others. C_p conditioning makes it difficult to connect your poor choices with the unpleasant outcomes in your life. Further, the lack of opportunity to make daily decisions for yourself makes it challenging to formulate plans and take initiative.

Climbing Up

For example, Luke told us about how he promised to meet Barry at the gate, to assist Barry start his new civilian life. But Luke was detained and unable to be there when Barry got out. Not knowing what to do, Barry got on a bus downtown and was robbed at the Greyhound station.

Barry was so bitter at Luke not being there to help him that Barry resumed criminal activity and went back to prison. The problem with Barry is that he blamed Luke for his circumstances rather than taking personal responsibility. Rather than adjusting to the situation, Barry depended too much on Luke. Barry allowed himself to become a victim by failing to have a back-up plan.

<u>Find a Christian Community</u>

Nowhere is this tendency more dangerous than when it comes to finding a Christian community. You must not expect others to be responsible for you. You must not blame others. God will provide for you, but you must take responsibility for yourself to join a group of Christian friends, start your new life, and stay committed to them. You need a Christian community to help you acclimate to civilian culture.

You may be wondering why we emphasize the need for Christian friends, when you may be more concerned about getting a job or a place to live. While it is obvious that you need to cover your physical needs, no job or home will help you make the cultural transition from prison to civilian life; *people do that.*

Think about this: if you were to travel to a new country, would you prefer to be given a *map* of the area, or would you rather be given a *personal guide?* Obviously, it would be better to have someone serve as a guide, someone who knows the geography and can help you get around. A group of Christian friends will be your guide to navigate any number of situations you face. They are more valuable that any job or housing situation or transportation. They will be more valuable than gold.

For example, after Bert's release, he went to dinner with some Christian friends. Bert was so thankful for the good meal he received that he started to enter the restaurant's kitchen to personally thank the chef. Bert was not aware he was about to break a rule of civilian culture, so his friends gently explained to him that there are other ways to express his gratitude to the chef.

Be Wary of Old Friends

Rather than being around believers, you may be tempted to associate with your old friends because they are more comfortable to be around. They may have been down themselves, or at least admire you for having been in prison. They know what you are going through, and give you a sense of meaning and identity. But they will not be the ones to help you re-enculturate properly in the new civilian culture, and they certainly will not help you grow in Christ. Instead, they are likely to lead you back into your old ways that resulted in your incarceration.

Find a Barnabas

Mark Walker talks about the example of Barnabas and Paul as it relates to your re-entry.[11] When Paul had come to Jerusalem, the believers were naturally reluctant to welcome the person who had murdered so many of their friends, skeptical about the genuineness of Paul's conversion. In the same way, you are an unknown person coming into a church family with a threatening history.

Climbing Up

What turned the tide of Paul's acceptance was the endorsement of Barnabas, a prominent and respected leader in their community (Acts 9:27). If you can develop a relationship with a Barnabas, he or she can testify to your faith in Christ. Having a trusted person to vouch for the integrity of your walk will reduce the barriers of fear and distrust, so other church members can get to know you more easily. A well-respected person in the church can be a bridge that accelerates your acceptance into their family.

Things to Consider about Church

1. There is no perfect church. People will let you down. It will not be like what you experienced in prison. Some may give you the impression that you are not welcomed, but in most cases, people will do their best to accept you. You may be misinterpreting their actions because you do not know how to read their culture. When you are tempted to leave and go somewhere else, or quit going to church altogether, do not give up! Stay connected.

2. Meet with one of the pastors or church leaders to disclose your history. Keep your meeting to an hour (remember pastors live in a hectic, busy culture). Humbly offer yourself to serve in any way. Do not promote yourself as a Bible teacher, preacher, or leader but come as a servant. If God wants to move you into greater responsibility, your service to the church over time will bear witness to your capacity, so leave that to God.

3. Find a church that teaches the Bible and has leaders who model Christlike behavior. Avoid signs of legalism, prosperity teaching, or rigid doctrines that cause disunity in the Body of Christ. These are legitimate reasons to leave and find another church.

4. Do not overwhelm the church with your needs. Ease into relationships by demonstrating concern for others. Be warm, loving, patient, and forgiving. Be humble enough to take on any

task. For example, you may want to teach, but be willing to clean the bathrooms, serve as a parking lot attendant, or play in the worship band.

5. Do not expect to earn a living in vocational ministry. These opportunities are rare and often take a long time before coming to fruition. It is most likely that you will serve bi-vocationally, like most Christians, working a "day job" and using your free time in ministry. Ask what the process is to become a leader in the church, understanding that you first need to demonstrate faithful servanthood. Ask how you can start small and work your way up to increasing responsibilities, such as an internship process.

6. Some churches may tell you bluntly that you are not welcomed there. Take it in stride and go to another church. While it is painful to face rejection, do not let the enemy use it to separate you from His people, wasting time watching TV or playing video games in isolation, as other returning citizens have done, to their peril. There <u>will</u> be a place that welcomes you and loves you, even if it takes a few tries.

Be Proactive

In prison it is normal and acceptable for inmates to ask for help for everything, even when they can do it themselves. It is a natural way of transacting business. Because of this C_p economic system, and the tendency to blame others, prisoners can succumb to a sense of entitlement.

Therefore, your inclination may be to ask church members to do things that you can do for yourself. For example, when Josh got out of prison, he asked people for rides and money, even when he could have secured a ride on the bus and had no immediate need for money. In a church with compassionate people, this can lead to manipulation and enabling.

Seek ways to solve your own problems before expecting others to take responsibility for you. Beware of asking for so much help that you wear people out. If you can get somewhere on foot or on the bus, you do not need to ask for a ride. Do the initial work of researching legal help or substance abuse programs, then ask for referrals for resources.

Also, be willing to accept help from a broad range of people so no one person or group gets burned out. If church members feel tapped out from your constant requests, resentment and fatigue can set in. Not understanding the cultural differences, you can be misunderstood as pushy, impatient, and demanding. Prove yourself to be innovative, determined, and proactive.

There is not much anyone can do for you if you will not help yourself. Do your part and do not blame others. Do not be a victim!

Listen to Others

In prison culture, you learned to trust no one. But in free-world culture, you must learn to trust if you want to thrive. While you must not be naïve, it is important to trust others, especially in the church. Grow in your ability to discern who is trustworthy, and consider their advice, especially when it is difficult to hear.

Remember that C_p culture distorts reality because of the lack of open dialogue. You may have fallen into "unique thinking," where you believe you are exempt from the rules that apply to others. Or you may have been deceived into believing that God has given you special insights and abilities that exempt you from the realities all other people must face.

You can recognize this in yourself when you think to yourself, "They just don't understand, my situation is different." When everyone else disagrees with you and you are the lone voice, it may reveal that you need to withhold judgment and listen.

You can also recognize warped thinking when you compare your sins to the sins of others. If you find yourself saying, "At least I didn't _____," this is a sure sign that you are justifying your actions. Jesus died for all sin and you are equally guilty, no matter what excuse or comparison you use to rationalize yourself.

God loves you as a unique individual, but you are not exempt from rules that apply to all humanity. Therefore, it is essential for you to find people who have different perspectives. They will provide a dose of reality to keep you from unrealistic notions resulting in disappointment.

Practice Patience

Another way to re-enculturate is to practice patience with time, others, and yourself.

With Time

Beware of the temptation to make up for lost time, expecting to accomplish everything at once. Some things take time. If you have unrealistic expectations that do not turn out as planned, you can quickly fall into despair, and even plunge into substance abuse. But if you will modify your expectations, you will not be disappointed,

Climbing Up

allowing you to shrug things off. God may be providing in different ways than you imagined.

With Others

Another way to practice patience is to wait before reacting to disrespect. Remember that C_p culture has trained you to respond immediately to signs of disrespect, without taking time to think it through.

Mitch told us a story that occurred over a year after his release. At a local restaurant, someone inadvertently cut in front of him in line and he barely caught himself before hitting the other person in the face. In his prison experience, if someone cut in front of him in the chow line, it was right to take immediate action. But this would have been inappropriate cultural behavior in free-world restaurants.

In these situations, it is normal to misinterpret harmless situations where you feel judged, condemned, or disrespected. For example, in prison it is offensive and threatening to stare at someone, and so this behavior is discouraged.

However, on the outside, someone may be looking off into the distance, not even looking at you. But because of your C_p experience, you may falsely take this as a sign of disrespect, escalating a harmless situation into a needless confrontation. When you think someone is intentionally disrespecting you, be slow to react before you confront.

With Yourself

Also, learn to be patient with yourself. After years in prison, your brain has been wired to thrive in a C_p environment. Upon release, your brain needs to be re-wired to adapt to the new culture. One of the ways your brain needs to adjust is to handle the bewildering number of options and decisions to make each day. Be patient with yourself as you develop new decision-making ability.

The process of re-enculturation can successfully end, but the process may not be steady. You may start well but then relapse. You may feel foolish and bewildered, like going through the teenage years again. But if you practice patience, after several months your brain will slowly get re-wired and you will function well just like everyone else.

Wait to Have a Platform

One of the dangers of re-enculturation is stepping into the limelight too fast. Many people will be thrilled to hear your testimony, your journey of transformation from prison to the outside world. Not understanding that you need time for cultural adjustment to civilian life, they will invite you to be on a platform to teach or share your testimony. This is a mistake.

Paul wisely cautioned Timothy against putting anyone in the public eye too early when he said, "Do not lay hands too quickly" (1 Tim. 5.22). Many former prisoners have been puffed up with pride by putting themselves on a pedestal for public adoration.

Civilians will romanticize your situation, not appreciating the temptation of pride when they treat you like a celebrity. You can become conceited like the devil, thinking "People want to hear me, I am the one who stirs people's hearts" (1 Tim. 3:6). When this happens, you become vulnerable to arrogance and a defiant spirit toward your leaders.

Climbing Up

Too Much Burden

The weight of sudden fame can also produce anxiety, insecurity, and doubt. You may think, "Can I maintain the current level of popularity or will I be abandoned? Maybe I should go back to my old friends who accept me as I am, where I don't have to be a celebrity." To help you cope with this burden, you may find yourself back in addictive behaviors.[12]

Alicia Chole said, "Over the decades, I have witnessed with tears the collapse of truly exceptional men and women who were crushed by the premature, combined weight of too much applause, too much authority, and too little self-control. So when I see those I mentor rushing toward the future or longing to be noticed or hungry for responsibility, I breathe a silent prayer: Oh, Jesus, grant them the gift of hiddenness. For a few more years, please let them grow in quiet anonymity."[13]

Your Response

Enter into a period of quiet, obscure service. Demonstrate faithfulness, just like everyone else in the congregation. Do not give your testimony in public for at least one year after your release. If you are invited to speak, politely decline by thanking the person and saying, "I have been counseled to wait a year before considering public speaking opportunities."

Of course, you can share God's work in your life in a small group or one-one setting, but even then, be aware of pride or drawing attention to yourself. After one year of faithful service, if you are invited to give your testimony publicly, get counsel from your leaders before accepting the invitation.

The Process of Re-enculturation

Continue to Grow in Christ

The last suggestion for re-enculturation is to continue growing in Christ. Former prisoners consistently report that they did well in their pursuit of Christ in prison but struggled to do so on the outside. The biggest factor is the busy schedule that returning citizens face.

On the inside, time moves slowly and prisoners are desperate to fill it with as many activities as possible. On the outside, time moves quickly and scheduling demands are constant, especially when trying to make up for lost time. Jerry told us that he had no time for church because he was working two jobs and had family obligations.

It can be easy to let daily time with God slip away because of other competing priorities. Even though you are no longer in C_p culture, you still need transformation from the habits of your old life. The effects of prison behavior may still be calling you: deceit, irresponsibility, aggressiveness, reckless disregard for others' safety, and the lack of remorse for the mistreatment of others.[14] If so, they must continually be replaced with Christlike behavior: honesty, responsibility, gentleness, prudence, obedience to authority, kindness, godly sorrow, and repentance.

Further, if you came from a from a broken family, an abusive situation, or a neglectful relationship, you must continue to press into Christ's healing in order to break those cycles of dysfunction.[15] This happens especially through practice of the spiritual disciplines, such as worshipping with believers in the church, reading and meditating on the Bible, prayer, and serving others through the church (see Appendix 5). Find people in the church who have been faithful for a long time and look to them as examples of a consistent walk.

Climbing Up

Conclusion

This chapter offered seven prescriptions for re-enculturation: take personal responsibility, find a Christian community, be proactive, listen to others, practice patience, wait a year for a platform, and continue to grow in Christ.

Questions for Reflection

1. Put the seven prescriptions for re-enculturation in rank order from easiest (1) to most difficult (7).

2. Talk to another person about these seven and ask that person to rank them from 1 to 7 and explain why.

3. For each of the seven prescriptions, make two lists of action items: 1) What you need to do while incarcerated; 2) what you need to do when you get out.

Chapter 7
Three Final Ideas

As you are Climbing Up, preparing yourself to make the cultural shift from prison to civilian life, there are three additional principles to consider. They will help you significantly as you leave the gates of prison.

3-3-3-12 Principle

The first principle has to do with intervals of time. Sports analysts propose there are certain strategic time periods where a team has an opportunity to gain a competitive advantage. In basketball, for example, the final four minutes before halftime is when a team can create momentum and demoralize the opponent going into the locker room.

In the same way, there are certain strategic moments in your re-entry that offer opportunity for confidence, but also leave you especially vulnerable to failure. Several prison ministers, including Clef Irby from Serving USA, have suggested four critical phases or time periods that can create a solid foundation for your re-entry.

3 Hours

The first phase is the *first three hours* upon release. This is when your new-found freedom can sweep you away and you can feel overwhelmed. This will pass, and you can get through it. But if you can arrange to have a Christian friend or family member meet you at the gate to spend those three hours with you, it will help you greatly.

3 Days

The next interval is the *first three days*. Again, having as much contact with Christian friends is wise because they can talk you through the adjustments you are facing. Spend much time in prayer, seeking the Lord and relying on Him to help you. Weathering these initial days will give you even more stability.

3 Months

The next time period is the *first three months*. Stay focused on the Lord, fellowship with His people, and stay disciplined in managing your time. Do not get discouraged when you need to adjust the plans you made while incarcerated.

12 Months

The final important phase is the *first 12 months*. With patient guidance and hard work, many former prisoners can adjust to civilian culture after one year, although it could easily take up to 24 months. The 3-3-3-12 Principle will help you pace yourself and see light at the end of the tunnel. Your mental transition from prison to civilian culture will take time, but it will be more difficult at the beginning than it is in the end.

Focus on one interval at time. Make it through the first three hours; then make it through the first three days; then be strong for the first three months. When you celebrate your 12-month anniversary of freedom, you may not be done, but you can be confident that you are well on your way to re-enculturation and fruitful work for the Lord in His Kingdom.

Double-Culture Shift

The second principle is what we call the "Double-Culture Shift." As already described in the preceding chapters, the first culture shift occurs when you are released and start re-enculturating from C_p to civilian culture (represented in following diagram):

Culture Shift

Original Culture		New Culture
Live, Work, Educated		Church

Urban Poverty: C_1

Mix Urban/Dominant Culture: C_2

Dominant Culture: C_3

ENCULTURATION

Prison Culture: C_p

- Decision making
- Constant vigilance
- Signs of disrespect
- Showing strength
- Distorted reality
- Constant interaction
- Bartering economy
- Persistent loss

RE-ENCULTURATION

Civilian Re-entry

But there may be a second potential cultural shift as well, and that has to do with a shift in *church* culture. Every church operates with its own set of unwritten rules. No church exists without rules of engagement. For example, one church may look down on a returning citizen with baggy pants, while another church is full of people with baggy pants. In prison, everyone speaks back to the preacher, shouting "Amen" or "Hallelujah" but other churches are more stoic, frowning on such responses during the preaching.

Wherever you end up in Christian community, you cannot escape the reality that there is a prevailing set of unspoken rules in that local church, and they are not always obvious. Awareness of that reality will help you adjust, but if you get caught off-guard the enemy can use this disequilibrium to cause you to quit going to church altogether.

Recall the discussion about American sub-culture (C_1, C_2, C_3), the cultural dynamics at work in American cities based on where someone lives, works, and educated. Church cultures are often associated to the C_1, C_2, C_3 culture in which they are connected.

Climbing Up

<u>Examples of the Second Shift</u>

For example, Joe is an Anglo who grew up in a blue-collar working poor family, with a white supremacist background (C_2 culture). Joe came to Christ in prison and experienced reconciliation with Blacks and Hispanics. His best friend was his African-American cellie who grew up in the inner-city (C_1 culture). He met volunteers from a C_3 suburban church who nurtured him in his faith.

When Joe is released, will he go to a C_1 culture church where his cellie came from? Will he go to the C_3 suburban church where the volunteers who discipled him go to church? Or will he go back to the all-white community where he grew up? Each church poses a different set of church cultural dynamics, based on their practices and heritage, and is likely to be dramatically different from his experience of church on the inside.

Another example is Andrea, a second-generation Hispanic woman who does not speak Spanish, even though she heard it growing up. She went to college and lived in a middle-class community before her arrest. She lived, worked, and was educated in C_3 culture. Will she go to a C_2 mixed-racially church that looks more like the church in prison? Or will she go to a C_3 church made up of people who share her background before incarceration?

Like Joe and Andrea, you may face the challenges of a double-culture shift (of civilian and church), which is illustrated on the right side of this diagram:

Double-Culture Shift

Original Culture Live, Work, Educated		**New Culture(s)** Civilian, Church
Urban Poverty: C_1	**Prison Culture: C_p**	**Civilian Re-entry**
Mix Urban/Dominant Culture: C_2	• Decision making • Constant vigilance • Signs of disrespect • Showing strength • Distorted reality • Constant interaction • Bartering economy • Persistent loss	**Church Re-entry** • C_1 • C_2 • C_3
Dominant Culture: C_3		

(ENCULTURATION → | ← RE-ENCULTURATION)

If you only have the shift from C_p to civilian culture, and you find a smooth transition into the culture of a local church, give thanks to God! But if you find it a challenge to fit in—first to civilian culture—and then secondly to a new church culture, do not be surprised. It is normal. You will get through it. Follow all the same advice given you in this book. Go back through and re-read the previous sections on re-enculturation, this time with a local church culture in mind. Doing so will help you prepare for the "Double-Culture Shift."

Handling Your Business

The final principle relates to the issue of handling your business. In C_p culture, handling your business immediately is the norm. The habit of quick, decisive action works in prison, but is arguably one of the most common causes of recidivism. This is because civilian culture views this kind of behavior as impulsive and rash. On the outside, people appreciate those who are calm in a tense situation, and feel threatened by what they interpret as impulsive behavior.

Climbing Up

For example, one returning citizen got a job in construction and watched in horror when a shouting match erupted between a Black supervisor and a Hispanic worker. Because of his C_p background, he expected this to escalate into a race war and he was not sure if he should jump in or just wait. His instinct was to engage, but before long the two finished their argument and went back to work as though nothing had happened.

This demonstrates how civilian culture is different than C_p, and why you need to learn how to resist impulsiveness. Instead of taking time to think through the wisdom of your situation, you may react too quickly. If someone insults you, do not immediately insult her back. Or if you see something you want to buy, resist the urge to purchase it on the spot until you are certain you have the money to pay for it.

Impulsiveness can be particularly discouraging if you experience a series of failed encounters with people. Before long, you may cascade into despair, believing you are a failure at everything. In the extreme, such discouragement has led people to give up their faith in God altogether.

Overcoming Impulsiveness

The deceiver has convinced millions of people that self-control is out of reach. Impulsive people bounce from one activity to another. They make resolutions, try drugs or hypnosis, or have surgery to gain control over their lives. In the end many sink even deeper into despair when nothing changes. It is difficult to overcome impulsiveness by will power alone. But change is possible.

Instead of becoming a victim, pay attention to those things you can control. To overcome impulsiveness, agree with these three truths:

1. I make my own choices.

2. I am responsible for my own actions.

3. I accept the consequences of my actions.

The most important way to gain victory over impulsiveness is to receive the grace of God and stop taking yourself so seriously. Spend more time in thanksgiving and praise, and less time ruminating over your failure. There is no condemnation to those who are in Christ Jesus (Rom. 8.1)! In Part II, we will explain in detail how to get victory over impulsiveness, as well as other areas of bondage.

Conclusion to Part I: Recognize the Culture

Culture assumptions are powerful because they are invisible. In fact, the rules of behavior are basic to all human functioning. We pray you recognize the cultural differences as you move from C_p culture to free-world culture.

Prison culture can be compared to civilian culture in terms of decision making, constant vigilance, signs of disrespect, showing strength, distorted reality, constant interaction, bartering economy, and persistent loss. These can clash with civilian culture through appearing unapproachable, holding to unwarranted fears, squandering new-found freedom, rejecting Christian community, and making up for lost time.

In your re-entry journey, you need a community of believers to help you re-enculturate, but do not wait for others. Instead be proactive, listen to others, practice patience, wait a year for a platform, and continue to grow in Christ. Finally, be aware of the *3-3-3-12 Principle*, the *Double-Culture Shift*, and the danger of impulsiveness.

Climbing Up

But above all, keep pushing yourself, day-by-day, beyond your comfort zone. If you persevere in Climbing Up, you can make it! Now that you understand how to recognize the culture, you are ready to learn about the next fundamental skill: Remember Your Identity.

Questions for Reflection

1. Think about the *3-3-3-12 Principle* and for each time period, list the dangers and opportunities you foresee for yourself upon release.

2. How might the *Double-Culture Shift* affect your re-entry experience as you adjust to life in Christian community?

3. Talk to three friends about how "handling your business" could be viewed as impulsiveness in civilian culture.

Part II: Remember Your Identity

"You have forgotten who you are and so forgotten me. Remember who you are."

– Mufasa, *The Lion King*

Chapter 8
The Father's Provision

NOW THAT YOU HAVE gained new understanding about prison culture
(C_p) and how it contrasts to civilian culture, you are ready to master
the next fundamental skill in re-entry: Remember Your Identity. In
this section, we will explain how God the Father makes provision
for your new identity, how Jesus created the potential you need
for abundant life, and how the Holy Spirit empowers you to be
transformed into your new identity in daily life.

Identity Dictates Behavior

Everyone has an identity, a way they understand themselves as
an individual, a group to which they belong, a role they play, or
a hobby they enjoy. For example, one person might say, "I am a
mom," another, "I am a Lakers fan," or, "I am a welder." But most
Americans understand themselves in terms of a *combination* of
several roles, groups, or interests.

Once you have an identity, it dictates how you spend your time
and what you think about. Moms spend their time differently than
welders, and Laker fans think about things differently than NASCAR
enthusiasts.

But some people are confused about their identity. You may have
heard the phrase, "I need to find myself." People say this when they
are unsure about who they are, their purpose in life. Their assumption
is, "If I can figure out my identity, I can live in accordance with it,
have a happy life, and be a whole person."

The danger in *finding your identity* in anything other than Christ is that
it can distract you from God's best for your life. Instead of *finding*

Climbing Up

your identity, the Father wants to *forge your identity* into the image of His Son Jesus (Rom. 8:29).

His way for you to experience true fulfillment is to allow Him to *forge your identity* to be like Jesus. Forging is a good description because it is a process where scrap metal is re-shaped into an instrument that is strong, durable, and useful. Therefore, the secret to a purposeful life is to surrender to the Spirit so He can forge you into the likeness of Christ.

Inherited Identity

At the moment of your salvation, as a follower of Jesus (see Appendix 7), you received God's spiritual DNA as His child. Since then He has been transforming you day by day to be more like Christ. So you do not need to "find yourself" as much as you need to "find out who you belong to." If you have received Christ's forgiveness and devoted your life to follow Him, you now belong to a King, with a cosmic Kingdom task that is larger than yourself, a spiritual identity that will shape your behavior.

This does not mean you lose your personality or distinctiveness. God will mold you into a unique person that is true to who you were created to be, an identity that is true to your real self. Like the superheroes of comic book fame, in Christ you discover your "true identity."

And as you allow God to forge your identity, you no longer have to "find yourself." You have been given a new start, a new nature, a new identity. You can stand on another soil, breath another air, and look up to another sky. Your life motives can change, making your inward drives brand new.

The wonder of all this is that God provides everything you need. You do not need to *find your identity*. Instead, you simply cooperate with God as He *forges your identity*. He will build your unique personality and gifting, making you into an increasingly productive ambassador for His Kingdom.

In other words, God forges, you participate.

A Happy Father

When you received Christ as Lord, you received a new Father. You were born of God and Jesus' DNA abides in you (1 Jn. 3:9). Your character is inherited from God the Father. This means you can spend your lifetime discovering your new family heritage.

Jesus expressed His confidence in the unbounded goodness and generosity of the Father who sent Him (Jn. 7:28-29). He is a loving Father who encourages His children (1 Th. 1:1), a generous parent who provides abundantly for us. Too often, people associate the Fatherhood of God with painful experiences of angry or distant human fathers, rather than Jesus' concept of the Father. The result is a twisted understanding that is out of sync with reality.

Our Father is lovable, radiant, happy, friendly, accessible, brimming with warmth, mercy, and kindness.[16] He is in total control, has complete competency, is the source of all life, and is the sustainer of all. His marvelous goodness is demonstrated in His attributes, perfect moral purity, absolute integrity, and unbounded love.[17]

Moreover, the Father shows concern for His creation, providing for every creature in a wondrously complex ecosystem where birds, fish, animals, and microorganisms flourish. The Father is gracious, offering His bounty to all people, even though no one deserves it. He shows a special compassion toward the needy and broken. He is slow to anger and patient in exercising judgment. His kindness leads people to repentance and salvation (Rom. 2.4).

<u>A Father We Can Trust</u>

When we fail to trust the goodness and provision of the Father, we can damage ourselves. Upon the examination of the many moral failures of well-known Christian leaders, what they have in common is a false assumption that "God has required me to take care of my own needs." When a person stops believing that the Father richly provides, the inevitable outcome is resentment toward God and a quest to find happiness alone. Therefore, the downfall of respected leaders is not rooted a desire for sex or power, but a lack of trust in the Father's good provision.[18]

But you can trust in the Father's goodness! Despite whatever circumstances you face, Rom. 8:35 reminds you that He is with you. Whether you face tribulation, distress, persecution, famine, nakedness, danger, or sword, no circumstances are beyond His redemptive purposes. Despite the attacks of Satan, you can be certain that the Father's unmerited favor is sufficient for all that you will face (2 Cor. 12:9).

<u>Designed to Adapt</u>

One way the Father demonstrates his generosity is through the adaptability that is found in His creation. He designed an amazing ability for living things to adapt in a changing environment. This is especially true in the highest of His creation: humankind, created in the image of God.

Recent scientific research in what is called "epigenetics" has shown how flexible God has made the human brain. Our brain is "neuroplastic," meaning it can change and grow. Not many years ago, the scientific community believed that once a brain was damaged, it could not be restored. But now, neuroscience has verified what Christians have known for years: we can be "transformed by the renewing of our minds" (Rom. 12:2).

The human brain is made up of physical, electromagnetic, quantum, and chemical activity that switches groups of genes in a positive or negative direction based on choices and beliefs we employ. When we believe damaging lies, they get wired into our genetic makeup, but they can also be wired back out by believing God's truth in their place.

Thinking destructive thoughts wires in toxic DNA that damages the body and the mind. On the other hand, DNA codes can be reversed by embracing thoughts of love, joy, appreciation, and gratitude. Because we are made in the image of God, we can stand outside our feelings and exercise control over the traffic of those thoughts. Like a person looking in through a window, we can observe a traumatic event and choose a healthy perspective based on God's truth. We can decide how to interpret the meaning of events and avoid being a victim of our circumstances.

Because of the Father's design, you are not stuck being the person you are today. While the genes you inherited do give you a predisposition to certain behaviors, they are not your destiny! Your thoughts and beliefs can change the structure of your brain at the molecular, genetic, and cellular level. The substance of toxic memories in your brain can be replaced with the truth of God's Word. The power of previous habits can be broken, because the Father has designed you to become a new person day by day!

An Imaginative Father

The Father is also the God of imagination. Imagination sees a universe of mysterious unknowns yet to be revealed, of complexity and wonder. Through the diversity of His creation, the Father's imagination is manifested everywhere we look.

The Father is free to act in creative, surprising ways. He provides rams stuck in thickets, makes ax heads float, and releases plagues that discredit the gods of Egypt. He sends his Son as a embryo in a Nazarene peasant girl and dispatches angels to visit lowly shepherds. He sends the Spirit to appear as tongues of fire at Pentecost and baffles religious leaders through uneducated apostles.

The Father is full of generosity, providing every good and perfect gift imaginable. He delights in His creation and rejoices in you. His sovereign rule can be felt like a warm ray of sunshine cracking through the clouds on a cold day.

Dallas Willard said, "We should think that God leads a very interesting life, and that He is full of joy. Undoubtedly, He is the most joyous being in the universe. The abundance of his love and generosity is inseparable from his infinite joy. All of the good and beautiful things from which we occasionally drink tiny droplets of soul-exhilarating joy, God continuously experiences in all their breadth and depth and richness."[19] He is an imaginative Father.

Designed for Imagination

The Father's imagination is further revealed in our own ability to practice imagination. Because we are meant to be perpetually creative beings, He devised a world that is conducive to our creative imagination and innovation. His earth is fully equipped to handle humanity's desire for creativity. Because we are made in the image of God, we are cut from the same cloth of the Father, having His imaginative nature within us. Therefore, we can look at our future like a person standing on the plateau of an open plain, with infinite possibilities before us and new adventures over the horizon.

Eph. 5:15-16 says "Look carefully then how you walk, not as unwise but as wise, making the best use of the time." The phrase "making the best use of the time" means to "buy up opportunities," which comes from the world of sailing (Latin for "toward the port"). The idea is that we need to be constantly aware of the winds and tides that shift one way or another, taking advantage of them to guide us toward the port.

To be wise is to recognize the winds and tides are more favorable at one time than another. So wisdom sometimes involves waiting. Other times it means acting quickly. I loved playing basketball because it requires constant assessment of opportunities. The best players make instantaneous decisions to pass, shoot, dribble, cut, or drive, depending on what is available. Even without the possession of the ball, a player is constantly observing the situation to take advantage of an opportunity that presents itself.

The Father has given us the gift of imagination so we can adjust to surprising situations. In the movie *Mission Impossible: Ghost Protocol*, Ethan wakes up to find himself in a Russian hospital bed. Waiting outside his room is a Russian agent ready to interrogate him.

Climbing Up

Without delay, Ethan uses his imagination. He steps out to the window ledge, high above the street, and assesses his options. Suddenly, as a truck appears below, he uses his belt to slide down a wire, lands on top of the passing truck, jumps off, and secures his escape through a crowd. Like Ethan, because we are created in the Father's image, we can employ imagination in difficult and confusing situations.

Conclusion

We can observe the Father's provision by giving us adaptability, imagination, and His remarkable creation. In addition, the Father provides for our daily needs, giving us confidence to press on. The Father wants to set you free to represent Him in the universe; first, by remembering who He is, then by living into your new nature. But in order for Him to forge you into your true identity, you need to cooperate with Him, believing he is a generous, happy, and trustworthy Father.

Questions for Reflection

1. Describe in your own words the difference between "finding your identity" and "forging your identity."

2. In what ways have you misunderstood the Father's nature?

3. Read Appendix 4: Bible Verses about your Identity in Christ. In what ways would your thinking and actions change if you could embrace the truth in these verses?

Chapter 9
The Son's Potential

THE FATHER HAS LAVISHED His benefits on all people. But the work of His Son Jesus has multiplied the Father's philanthropy so we can experience even more of His goodness in this fallen world. The Father had always intended to restore the brokenness of creation through Jesus by revealing "to us the mystery of His will, according to His purpose, which He set forth in Christ as a plan for the fullness of time, to unite all things in Him, things in heaven and things on earth" (Eph. 1:9-10). In Christ, the Kingdom of God the Father has come!

Because of Jesus, we have SWAG (Stuff-We-All-Get) including adoption, holiness, forgiveness, insight, intimacy, assurance, belonging, hope, power, meaning, creativity, individuality, community, and an inheritance (Eph. 1-3). Through frequent references to "in Him," Paul reminds us that it is only by Christ's work that we possess this wide array of blessing, and he caps it off with this crescendo: "To Him be glory in the church and in Christ Jesus throughout all generations, forever and ever. Amen" (Eph. 3:21).

Reservoir of Potential

Jesus is like a vast reservoir of living water for a thirsty world. He said, "The water that I will give him will become in him a spring of water welling up to eternal life" (Jn. 4:14). But without Christ's victory over the devil, there would be no reservoir from which we could draw. He won several victories over the enemy: in His temptation; through His healings, teachings, exorcisms; by His righteous obedience to the Law; through His death, burial, and resurrection; through His ascension to rulership on the throne.

Climbing Up

His complete victory grants Him a level of authority that emboldens us to teach others to obey His commands (Mt. 28:18-20). He transferred us from the domain of darkness into His Kingdom of light (Col. 1:13-14) and sent the Spirit to indwell us. Because of Jesus, we have a constant source of living water to extinguish fires of despair, to create, to bless, and to protect. He is the source, but we are the instruments that Christ uses to deliver His grace.

Because we are in Christ, we have new confidence that our efforts have eternal value (Eph. 4:7-12). Therefore, He invites us to continue His work, by being "strong in the Lord and the strength of his might" (Eph. 6:10). His abundant potential can be multiplied on the earth for the benefit of others. Prosperity teachers talk about blessing for their *own* personal consumption, but Jesus wants to bless *others* through us. We are God's workmanship, His creative expression, created for good works in Christ Jesus (Eph. 2:10), to bear fruit on His behalf (Jn. 15:1-8), doing even greater works than He did (Jn. 14:12).

Because of the reservoir that Jesus possesses, we can pass along His grace in the form of hope, comfort, and encouragement to those confused by the accuser's lies and schemes. He gives us the ability to draw near to others who are in pain, rather than retreat in fear. Because Jesus is our source, we come with living water of deliverance and joy, not condemnation and fear. We can help other believers find their gifts and calling so they reach their full potential.

The world defines a person's value through money, education, experience, power, or influence. Without such advantages the world declares that person to be without value. But Jesus said that God could use anyone in His Kingdom: the poor, those who mourn, the meek, those who hunger and thirst for righteousness, the merciful, the pure in heart, the peacemakers, and the persecuted (Mt. 5:3-12).

Seeking Approval

Jesus can work in us but we put obstacles in our own way. Perhaps the biggest obstacle to forging our identity in Christ is our desire to win the approval of people. The impulse to be important is not evil. On the contrary, it is a quality embedded in us by God himself. He wired us to be creative, to do things that matter, to be noticed and appreciated. Humans are built to be indispensable.

But the devil takes advantage of this desire, hoping we will put all our effort into securing the approval of others. In a fallen world, the God-given drive to be significant can be twisted into an obsession to get attention or become famous. Wondering if we really count, we are terrified about being worthless. So we frantically pour ourselves into activities to address our fear of insignificance.

Throughout the history of human civilization, people have dedicated most of their physical and emotional energy to taking credit and avoiding blame, maximizing pleasure and minimizing pain. We devote ourselves to appearing right in others' eyes, hiding our inadequacies, and promoting our own success.

Ivory Towers and City Streets

No one escapes the temptation to seek approval. The gangbanger running the streets wants to impress his posse. The college professor covets approval from other academics. Each one wants to stand out among their peers, desiring honor and recognition. Everyone pursues the esteem of their little crowd, even though they differ on how to achieve that respect.

Climbing Up

The worst condition we can imagine is to be invisible and insignificant. Children will do anything to avoid that kind of obscurity, even act in self-destructive ways. All through life, people do desperate things to be noticed, respected, and honored.

James warned: "You desire but do not have, so you kill. You covet but you cannot get what you want, so you quarrel and fight. You do not have because you do not ask God. When you ask, you do not receive, because you ask with wrong motives, that you may spend what you get on your pleasures" (Js. 4:2-3). We long to be noticed, no matter the cost.

Since Jesus overcame this temptation to be famous, we can take on His identity, finding increasing freedom by living into our spiritual DNA. Our fears to win "the approval of people" can be changed to enjoying "the approval of God." Because Jesus won this battle, He secured the potential for us to win this battle too.

Winning the battle of people-pleasing will require victory in four areas:

1: Believe You are Adequately Loved

The first area is to believe, like Jesus did, that you are adequately loved by God the Father. This is more than a theological acknowledgment about of God's character. It is a heartfelt, rock-solid conviction that God delights in you and is pulling for you. God's adoring eyes have always been upon you. You had His attention all along, but you could not see it because you were too distracted by the sight of yourself.

You must be certain that 2 Pet. 1:3 is true: "You have been given everything you need for life and godliness." This means you can walk in safety and security, confident of God's work in human history.

You can breathe a sigh of relief because you do matter. You are significant. You do not have to earn others' acceptance, because you are already accepted. You belong!

Many people get stuck here because they cannot accept God's forgiveness. You may live in a constant state of guilt and bondage because you do not really believe that Christ's blood is sufficient to cover your sins. But if you have confidence that Christ paid the price for all your wrongdoing, you can confess it, receive forgiveness, and quickly move on (1 Jn. 1:9).

Knowing you are loved frees you from the fear of failure. Instead, you can step into an adventuresome life because the risk is low and the reward is high. Your labor in the Lord is not in vain (1 Cor. 15:58). God never leaves you or forsakes you (Heb. 13:5). He does not leave you as an orphan (Jn. 14:18). Because God has minimized the risk, you are set free to pursue the heroic efforts of any enterprise He assigns to you.

2: Take on Boring and Thankless Tasks

The second area is an eagerness to do boring and thankless tasks. Most people consider themselves above the gritty and relentless details, so they are unwilling to pursue what seems "beneath them." They say things like, "I didn't do four years of college to do that." God resists the proud but gives grace to the humble (Js. 4:6).

You may have a death grip on that which defines you: work, family, sexuality, ethnicity, or ministry. Tozer said, "We need to have taken from our dying hand the shadow scepter with which we fancy we rule the world."[20]

Climbing Up

3: Release Bitterness

The third area is to forgive others and not see them as enemies. When you refuse to forgive others, your mind is enslaved to bitterness. This is why Jesus taught us to pray that God would forgive us our sins as we forgive those who sin against us (Mt. 6:12). If you believe that others are blocking your potential or stifling your goals, you can lose sight that God is still in control.

You may think, "My PO is against me, my leaders are shortsighted, my friends don't understand me, my boss is jealous, and my spouse is dragging me down. The old-timers shut down new ideas, and the young people do not respect the wisdom of elders."

Is the Lord really so weak that He cannot overcome these challenges? Is He unaware of your frustration? Is He asleep on the job? Without question, you are affected by the decisions of others, but they are not the ones holding you back. There is only one person who can destroy your future. That person is you. You are the only one who can sabotage your potential by nurturing a bitter spirit. You can decide to joyfully trust God in spite of your frustration.

4: Embrace Obscurity

The final area is taking up your cross as Jesus commanded (Mt. 16:24). The way of Jesus is obscurity first, exaltation second. Good-Friday crucifixion comes first, Easter-Sunday resurrection comes later.

Don learned this principle early in his life, working for a difficult boss. This employer resisted employee ideas unless he could take credit for them himself. And even when he did endorse one of the worker's proposals, he frequently declared publicly that they were his own ideas.

For a long time this was a source of aggravation for Don. He would offer up innovative solutions only to have them disapproved for no reason, or worse yet, hear about them being implemented without receiving proper recognition. But for the good of the company, Don slowly learned to release his frustration, allowing his boss to receive notoriety for the implementation of Don's ideas.

As he embraced obscurity, Don found new satisfaction with his work and discovered increasing imagination to generate even more new innovative ideas. He saw the fulfillment of 1 Pet. 5:6-10 happen before his eyes: "He himself will restore, strengthen, establish, and confirm you." The obscurity of the cross was Jesus' way, and it is the way for us too. When you humble yourself under God's mighty hand, He will lift you up at the proper time.

Conclusion

You can be reshaped and forged into a nozzle that delivers living water from the Christ-reservoir, offering refreshment to thirsty people in need. When you are released from the bondage of seeking approval, His life-giving potential can flow through you. The Father demonstrated His philanthropic heart by sending the Son to provide you with potential for doing good so you can bring refreshment to the world.

Questions for Reflection

1. Of the four areas needed to escape people-pleasing, which one is the most difficult? How will you accept this truth so God can forge your identity to be like Christ?

Climbing Up

2. What does it mean that Jesus came to give you potential? List three things you have the ability to do because of His works (such as His life, teaching, death, resurrection, or ascension).

3. Read all the passages referenced in this chapter and choose one to memorize to help you remember your identity in Christ.

Chapter 10
The Spirit's Power

THE FATHER IS OVERFLOWING in loving provision. The Son has achieved the victory over the devil, creating abundant potential for us to do good. But God does not stop at provision and potential. He also gives us power by the Holy Spirit! When people in the Bible were filled with the Spirit, it resulted in action: they spoke, they protected, or they defended. The Spirit initiates action, giving *power to accomplish something.*

Look at the frequent references to the word "power" in describing the Spirit's work:

> "I pray that out of his glorious riches He may strengthen you with power through his Spirit in your inner being, so that Christ may dwell in your hearts through faith. And I pray that you, being rooted and established in love, may have power, together with all the Lord's holy people, to grasp how wide and long and high and deep is the love of Christ, and to know this love that surpasses knowledge-that you may be filled to the measure of all the fullness of God. Now to Him who is able to do immeasurably more than all we ask or imagine, according to his power that is at work within us" (Eph. 3:16-20, emphasis added).

The Spirit gives power to exercise self-control (2 Tim. 1:7), be His witnesses (Acts 1:8), overcome weakness (Rom. 8:26), gain wisdom and knowledge about God (Eph. 1:18, 3:4-6, 16-19, 2 Pet. 1:21), engage in battle (Is. 28:6), and remember what Jesus taught (Jn. 14:26). He leads us into truth (Jn. 16:13, 2 Thess. 2:13). The Spirit refreshes us (Jn.7:38-39) by setting our minds on life and peace (Rom. 8:6). By His power He raises us from the dead (Rom. 8:11) and gives us the ability to be free from obedience to the flesh (Gal. 5:16).

Climbing Up

From the Holy Spirit we have weapons for our warfare (Eph. 6:10-20) and supernatural gifts to serve others (1 Cor. 13, Rom. 12, 1 Pet. 4). He fills us with joy, thanksgiving, and mutual submission (Eph. 5:18-21), and is the guarantee of our future inheritance (Eph. 1:13-14, 4:30). The Spirit provides access to the Father (Eph. 2:18) and is building us into a dwelling place for God (Eph. 2:22).

Making Us One

The Holy Spirit is also the "Great Integrator," bringing various scattered people and factions into a single Body of Christ. The Spirit integrates the Body to the Head (Eph. 2:15-16, 4:11-16, Col. 1:28). He builds us into one Temple of the Spirit by disciplining, strengthening, gifting, comforting, and encouraging the members.

The Holy Spirit is constructing a Christ-centered, fully functioning Body, with a diversity of operating members. Believers are equipped for ministry as the Body grows in unity and knowledge of the Son of God, where each person becomes mature like Jesus. He helps us develop coordination so we have a self-replicating quality, building up the Body in love (Eph. 4:12-16).

Like a great music conductor, He orchestrates the Body of Christ to function in harmony, according to the creative vision of the Composer. He takes our various gifts and knits them together for increasing functionality.

Bridging the Gap

The Spirit bridges the gap between Jesus' first and second appearances to earth. The gospel narrative reached an important climax at Jesus' resurrection and ascension. But God's work continued with the Spirit's coming at Pentecost. Between Jesus's incarnation and His

Return, the Spirit now superintends the work of Christ on earth. At Pentecost, the Third Person of the Trinity dramatically became the link between Christ's first and second comings, beginning a new and intimate relationship with us, the Church.

The Spirit is now our constant companion in the Already (the Kingdom has come), and the Not-Yet (the Kingdom is not fully evidenced in this sinful age) Kingdom. The Spirit helps us live in the tension of the "already/not-yet Kingdom," where we have a foretaste of eternity but still endure the suffering of this life on earth. He gives us power to live in constant anticipation of Jesus' return, giving us courage to persevere. The Spirit is tangible evidence that the treasures of eternity are given to us right now AND a guarantee that He will see us through to completion.

By animating, encouraging, and empowering us, He reminds us that the responsibilities of life do not fall on us alone. We cooperate with the Spirit because it is our destiny to be valiant and triumphant until Christ returns. We get busy because He motivates us to do God's work.

Jesus was conceived by a work of the Spirit, with the willing cooperation of Mary. In the same way, the Spirit impregnates the Church to do the works of God. He motivates, inspires, and directs, but only with our cooperation. In short, the Spirit helps us accomplish tasks, but not in our own strength.

The Emblem

Another way the Spirit empowers us is by serving as the emblem, or evidence, that we are the people of God. After the Exodus, Israel was distinct among the nations by its identification with God through the Law of Moses. The Law was a visible emblem showing they belonged to God. Because the Law was given after their deliverance from Egypt, God demonstrated His salvation by grace from day one. The Law was a gift to help them function as the people of God, a visible reminder of His presence with them.

But now the Law has served its purpose and has been replaced by the Spirit. He is the new evidence of our adoption, reminding us that we are a people belonging to God. The Spirit replaced the Law as a better and more permanent gift. The Law was a wonderful source of guidance for the people of God, but its use was temporary (Gal. 3:24). The Spirit is a better emblem in that we are given power to obey, not just instruction on how to live.

The Spirit's Return on Investment (ROI)

When you were born again, you received a new identity, a new nature designed to bear fruit for His Kingdom. You are designed to produce a return on God's investment (ROI). Like a venture capitalist, God supplies you with resources and then equips you to do something good with it.

A venture capitalist is an investor who provides money for entrepreneurs who do not have the capital to get started in business. By releasing venture capital to an entrepreneur, blessings are multiplied in a community. People are hired, goods are purchased, new businesses are generated who then hire even more employees. An investor's provision multiplies benefits in a society.

In the same way, God invests in you to multiply abundance of blessing for the world. In the Kingdom, spiritual wealth creation is achieved through spiritual entrepreneurs, stewards who cleverly take what God provides to innovate, experiment, adjust, toil, assess, and innovate again. By doing so, they produce a Kingdom ROI.

Innovations cannot be planned or predicted because they emerge from the daring vision of an entrepreneur. In business, we know about the imagination of Steve Jobs (Apple), Mark Zuckerberg (Facebook), or Sam Walton (Walmart). In sports, fans marveled at the ingenuity of Michael Jordan (basketball) or Bill Belichick (football).

In the Kingdom, imagination has been displayed by Bill Bright, Martin Luther King, and John Wesley. God's design is to realize his venture capital return through your life. When your imagination is unleashed, you have ability to innovate, seizing opportunities as they arise.

Jesus and the Apostles' Teaching

When you consider the themes of Jesus' parables, you will see that this is true. God gives talents and expects to receive back more than He put in. He provides the seed and expects 30, 60, 100 times the investment. A small seed produces a large plant that provides refuge for others, a small amount of leaven spreads to whole loaf, and healthy trees bear good fruit (Mt. 7:17, 12:33, 13:31-33, 19:3-9, 25:14-30).

Jesus and the apostles refer to multiplication throughout the Gospels and Epistles. For example, an investment in a winepress had the expectation of a profit, a farmer planted a fig tree looking for a return, a grain of wheat falls and dies in order to multiply into more grain, and God prunes like a vinedresser in order to produce more fruit—fruit that remains (Mt. 21:33-41, Lk. 13:6-8, Jn. 12:24,15:2, 16). He expects us to produce a harvest of righteousness and other fruit of the Spirit (Js. 3:17-18, Heb. 12:11, Gal. 5:22-23).

Principles of ROI

The question is not whether we should produce a return on investment, but how. It is produced through time, effort, failure, and courage.

Climbing Up

Time

The first principle of producing good return on investment is that it takes a long time to produce: Mt. 25:19 says, "Now after a long time the master of those servants came and settled accounts with them." The effective stewards, those who doubled the venture capital given to them, took a long time to achieve that return. They did not pursue "get rich quick" schemes.

You must wait in expectation that God will give wisdom, but maybe not on your timetable: "They that wait upon the Lord will renew their strength (Is. 40:31)." This is not a despairing waiting, but an expectant waiting, a peaceful waiting. God is at work while you wait. <u>ROI takes time.</u>

Effort

The second principle is that ROI takes effort. It demands discipline, ambition, and courage. God is pleased when you try and fail but displeased when you play it safe, burying his treasure in the ground. The lazy steward was right to say: "I knew you are a hard man, harvesting where you have not sown and gathering where you have not scattered seed (Mt. 25:24)."

God wants you to be diligent, using your imagination so He can receive a return on his investment. He wants to receive harvest, but He wants you to sow the seeds. He expects you to be clever and work hard to get the job done. <u>ROI takes effort.</u>

Failure

The third principle is that ROI involves *failure*. Many ideas you attempt will not work, some at a laughable level. But God can redeem everything. Innovators value failure because they learn from it. A plant that goes to seed can be the source of a plentiful harvest in the future, so you should cast seed and see what comes up. What seems like a spark of genius might fall flat. Then to your surprise, a different approach suddenly works. Some of our best ideas have come upon second and third attempts. <u>ROI takes failure.</u>

Courage

When you aspire to yield an ROI for God, it is more about bravado than technique, more about courage than information, and more about confidence than procedure. It is not just studying the Bible, it is applying biblical truth in creative situations, trusting in Him to bring the fruit that glorifies His name.

Just like businesspeople do when they are endowed with venture capital, your identity as a follower of Christ makes you qualified to initiate creative ideas in complex spiritual situations. You can exploit gospel opportunities quickly and adjust to discouraging setbacks. <u>ROI takes courage.</u>

Prisoners have told us their creative ideas for outreach in prison that illustrate this idea. One of our favorites is a group of prisoners who received permission to set up a burrito bar on the yard. They purchased the food and handed it out to everyone as an opportunity to demonstrate and declare the love of Christ.

Conclusion

You are fearfully and wonderfully made in the image of God (Ps 139:14, Gen. 1:28). You are his workmanship, created in Christ Jesus to do good works which God prepared beforehand, so you can walk in them (Eph. 2:10). By the Spirit, you are being transformed into the image of Christ from one degree of glory to another. (2 Cor. 3:18).

Climbing Up

The Spirit makes us one, bridges the gap, and is the emblem of our identity as the people of God. He is integrating us to the Head (Jesus), making us function together as a mature Body, so we serve as an agent of grace in this fallen world. Through us, He is progressively advancing His Kingdom on earth as it is in heaven.

Spiritual warfare is not the frightening encounters seen in movies, but the day-to-day grind of cooperating with the Spirit who gives you power to be forged into the identity of Christ. This power is not just an occasional burst of energy, but a supernatural ability to change at a molecular level, to become a transformed person. The Spirit of Truth leads us into the truth that makes us free (Jn. 8:32, 14:16-17).

The Father's philanthropy, the Son's potential, and the Spirit's power are given to you by grace, with eager anticipation to see how you will produce a return on His investment.

Questions for Reflection

1. What does it mean that the Spirit gives us power? List three things you are able to do because the Holy Spirit came to His people.

2. As you think about God as a Venture Capitalist, what resources did He give you so you could live out your identity as a spiritual entrepreneur?

3. Which of the four principles of ROI will take the most effort to apply?

Chapter 11
Your Identity Is Under Siege

THE FATHER HAS LAVISHED you with spiritual potential through the work of Jesus Christ, empowered by the Holy Spirit. Because you share in His nature, you have a new identity, a new ability to produce a return on God's investment. You can bring Him glory, representing Him as an ambassador to a hurting world. God forges, you participate.

But there is another player in this process, an enemy who lies to you about who you are, an adversary who attempts to destabilize you. He would like to frame the debate of your identity so you forget who you are. In *The Lion King*, Mufasa told his son Simba, "You have forgotten who you are and so forgotten me. Remember who you are." When you forget who you are, you forget who God is too.

The devil does not care what identity you pursue, as long as you forget your true identity in Christ. So, if you base your identity on being a respected gangbanging drug lord, Satan wins. But he also wins if your identity is based solely on being a law-abiding accountant. Identities do not have to be overtly evil to be distracting, they simply need to keep you from your true identity as an ambassador of Christ.

From Blinding to Distraction

Before you knew Christ, you were blinded to the truth. But now God has opened your eyes to the gospel. When you crossed over from death to life, the deceiver lost you forever to the Kingdom of Light. Because of that defeat, he turns all his energy to tricking you into squandering the treasures God provides. He pivots from keeping you <u>blinded</u> to keeping you <u>distracted.</u>

Climbing Up

He wants to mess with your mind so you do not live as a true child of God. He puts down his weapons of blinding and picks up new weapons of distraction, disruption, and discouragement. Jesus called him "the father of lies" (Jn. 8:44). Luther said, "For still our ancient foe doth seek to work us woe, his craft and power are great, and armed with cruel hate, on earth is not his equal."

On one side, God is constantly providing truth, encouragement, and comfort to make us increasingly fruitful, so we can produce a return on His investment. On the other side, the evil one works every day to work against what God is doing. No one is exempt from his methods, and no one can live a single day without being in the middle of this spiritual confrontation.

Lies Can Seem Real

How does this happen? The deceiver tells us lies that seem to be true.

We had not been married long when a cold draft of air woke Cathy from her slumber. Looking up, she saw Don slowly pulling the covers off the bed. She said, "What are you doing?!" Don abruptly whispered, "Shhhhhh. There's a snake in the bed." She said, "You are dreaming, give me the blankets back and go to sleep." Cathy made several earnest attempts to assure Don of their safety before he finally gave the covers back to her. It took a while before Don came to his senses and realized it was all a dream.

This is how the enemy deceives us in real life. All of us are subjected to lies and feelings that have only partial connection to reality. Satan's lies seem real and based on sound experience. Don really thought there was a snake in the bed, and so his adrenaline was pumping at the same rate as if a snake were really in the bed. His body reacted as though the delusion was true.

In the same way, your body cannot tell the difference between truth and lies. If you hear a lie enough times and you start to believe it, your body will react with the same destructive power as though it were true. For example, if you accept the lie, "God has abandoned you and you are alone," your body will suffer anxiety leading to bitterness, worthlessness, disappointment, and fear (even though God has not abandoned you and you are not alone).

Expose Lies and Affirm Truth

What can you do in the face of these insidious lies? Your job is to expose lies and affirm truth. Lies and truth have no power in themselves; they are neutral. You activate lies or truth by what you choose to believe. You can expose the lies of the deceiver and affirm the truth of God's Word.

When you repeatedly fall for the same lies, they form toxic habits and attitudes, and you start living in a constant state of panic. Whenever you agree with the devil's deceptions, you etch grooves in your brain that eventually result in strongholds. On the other hand, if you believe what God's Word says, the Spirit etches grooves in your brain to make you more like the Lord Jesus. When you agree with the truth of God's word, you demolish old strongholds and forge new habits that bring life and peace.

You can change from the inside out, being forged to become more like Jesus. This means you do not need to "try harder to avoid sin," but by the forging work of the Spirit, you can be transformed to be a different person from the inside out.

111

Climbing Up

The adversary employs schemes to get us to forget our identity, dump our treasured possessions in Christ, and abandon our faith in God. But we are not left powerless against those schemes. In fact the Bible teaches that "the weapons of our warfare have divine power" (2 Cor. 10:4) so that we can stand against the schemes of the devil (Eph. 6:10-20).

Two Sides

John 10:10 provides a basic template to understand the Christian life. Jesus said about the enemy, "The thief comes only to steal and kill and destroy" (Jn. 10:10a). He is a pillager, a robber, and a murderer. He attempts to thwart God's work and ruin our lives at the same time. Jesus offered "Part B" to John 10:10, by saying He came that we might have life and have it abundantly. The thief steals, kills, and destroys but Jesus gives abundant life.

Sometimes we miss the violent nature of Satan's agenda. Jesus did not say he comes to "tickle, bump, and annoy" but to "steal, kill and destroy." He is a vicious and powerful adversary prowling around for someone to devour (1 Pet. 5:8). His objective is chaos and devastation.

But Jesus came to destroy the works of the devil (1 Jn. 3:8). He countered Satan's chaos and devastation by empowering us to be His ambassadors so we could also destroy the devil's works. C.S. Lewis talked about this idea by saying Jesus was like a King who landed in disguise and invited us to join in a great work of sabotage.[21] As the people of His story, God uses us to carry on this work of sabotage. This is the cosmic campaign, and you are in the middle of it.

The Battleground: Your Mind

The location of this cosmic John 10:10 campaign between the evil one and Jesus is the <u>battlefield of your mind</u>. The enemy looks at you through the crosshairs of his weapons scope, because if he can rule your mind, he can keep you from being effective for Christ. And he does so with a three-step, progressive strategy: devaluing, amplifying, and hyperbolizing.[22]

Devaluing

The accuser starts by speaking words of insecurity that strike at your fears: failure, what others think, rejection, disrespect, poverty, loneliness, you name it. The accuser one analyzes you, sizes you up, and designs a personalized line of attack that plays on your fears. Do any of these devaluing messages sound familiar?

- You do not belong.

- No one loves you so you are lonely and miserable.

- You have no talent or gifting so there is no hope for you.

- Look at her, why can't you be like her?

- God does not really love you or this bad thing would not have happened.

- You are not really a Christian—look at what you just did.

- You will never change.

Every day you are bombarded by the incessant, constant pounding of lies to get you to devalue yourself. In fact, he disguises his messages to make them appear to be your own ideas, not his. Designing a personalized attack strategy, he chips away at you. He knows what is effective on Jim will not work on Susie, and what works on Susie will not work on Frank. Every person has enough fears for the evil one to formulate an effective, individualized devaluation strategy. But devaluing is just the first step.

Amplifying

Once you agree with his devaluing lies, he has gained a foothold and will proceed to amplify your situation to make it worse:

- Since you failed this time, you will <u>always</u> fail.

- Since you feel lonely now, you will <u>always</u> feel lonely.

- Since you are divorced, <u>no one</u> will ever love you again.

- Since your spouse yelled at you, you will <u>never</u> have a good marriage.

- <u>Nothing</u> goes right with you, <u>everything</u> you touch fails.

Amplifying occurs when a legitimate fear is exaggerated. For example, consider a young person so burdened with anxiety that she cannot go out to find a job. She wants employment but says, "I've tried but I can't. I hate interviews. They scare me."

When asked what scares her, she says, "They might look down on me and make me feel foolish. That would be terrible. It would be horrible." The truth is, it would not really be the end of the world if someone viewed her as foolish. It would be unpleasant, but not the end of the world. The devil is amplifying her fears and she is buying it.

Consider two unnecessary burdens with amplifying. First, the dreaded circumstances may never occur, so there is wasted anxiety over something that might not happen. Second, even if it does happen, it is rarely as bad as it was imagined to be. The enemy has a field day generating troubling scenario after troubling scenario, watching us add fuel to the fire of his lies.

Once you believe his amplifying efforts, he will move to the next phase: blow up the lie to an absurd, irrational level, called "hyperbole."

Hyperbolizing

Here are a few examples of hyperbole that enter into the realm of the absurd:

- I need to be perfect *all the time*, or I will *never* get respect.
- *Everyone* is against me, *all the time*.
- If I do not meet *everyone's* expectations, I will *never* have friends.
- Since I do not have a boyfriend/girlfriend right now, my life is *over*.
- I will never make it in life; it is *hopeless*.
- Why even try?

When his lies are presented and you receive them without cross-examination, they form an attitude. Over time, as you continue believing lies these attitudes become a normal part of your thinking. If you repeatedly believe his devaluing lies, then amplify them, and allow them to blow up to a hyperbolic level, you construct a stronghold that is difficult to demolish.

Therefore, by your acceptance of his lies, a stronghold is built one thought at a time. The effect of a stronghold takes on many forms: anxiety, depression, mental illness, physical maladies, broken relationships, and even suicide.

Climbing Up

Conclusion

The deceiver never takes a day off. He never leaves anyone alone. Since he had the audacity to tempt the Lord Jesus with lies, you can be sure he will not leave you alone either. You can be a secure and godly person, but he will keep throwing false messages at you every day. No one can escape the accuser's intrusion into their thoughts.

Therefore, you need to realize that not every thought that pops in your head is true. Not every thought has to be passively accepted or actively ratified. You do not have to be victimized by the evil one any more than Don needed to believe there was a snake in the bed. You do not have to entertain every idea that invades your mind. God has a better way. He provides insight about the schemes of the devil (2 Cor. 2:11), so you can recognize deception and choose the truth.

Questions for Reflection

1. Think about three examples where you experienced devaluing, amplifying, or hyperbolizing.

2. How might your physical body have been affected by believing lies over a long period of time?

3. What are three strongholds that have been established by forgetting your identity in Christ?

Chapter 12
Recognizing Satan's Schemes

YOUR IDENTITY IN CHRIST cannot be taken from you. But you can be tricked into believing lies that cause doubt about your identity, leading you to self-destructive activities. Therefore, it is important to be aware of the schemes of the devil so you can reject his lies and walk in God's truth.

Two Scheming Metaphors

To understand Satan's schemes, it is helpful to remember his goal. Evil spirits are constantly at work to trick us into giving away our treasures. They want us to relinquish our valuables by our own free will. Their activities can be understood using two familiar metaphors: rodents and con artists.

Rodents

Demons are like rats in that they need garbage to feed on. When you leave garbage unattended in your life, you give evil spirits an entry point, an invitation to make matters worse. When you let worry, lust, greed, and bitterness pile up inside, they become like a growing pile of trash that invites infestation (Eph. 4:27). Do not give spiritual forces of evil an opportunity to get a foothold in your life.

To get rid of rats, the trash has to be taken away. As each bit of refuse is removed, you discourage future infestations. The adversary knows that whatever you meditate on will grow, for good or bad. If you interpret events in light of God's Word, you remove trashy thoughts, resulting in comfort and peace. But if you allow the enemy to narrate your circumstances, disconnected from the bible, you permit the decaying pile of garbage to grow, resulting in even more damage.

Climbing Up

Rats prefer to invade at night, where they cannot be seen. In the same way, Satan likes to keep you unaware of his activities. When you resist him, bringing the truth into the light, he will flee (Js. 4:7).

Con Artists

Another metaphor of the pillaging deceiver is the confidence artist (aka con artist). By designing elaborate schemes that draw people into their confidence, they give a victim (aka the mark) an opportunity to hand over their wealth voluntarily.

A contemporary scheme is where the con artist sends an email, portraying herself as a distraught family member, caught overseas without funds. The con artist asks a grandmother or uncle to wire money to a foreign account that will presumably rescue the suffering family member. But the funds are actually routed to the con artist's bank account, never to be seen again.

Since the devil cannot rob you at gunpoint, cannot harm you without God's permission, and cannot take away your salvation in Christ, the best he can do is trick you into *voluntarily discarding your riches*. He knows you have a rich inheritance through Jesus Christ that is untouchable. But he also knows he can trick you to voluntarily exchange your joy, confidence, or trust in God for short-term popularity, success, or pleasure.

Your identity is under constant siege. He tries to steal, kill, and destroy the identity that the Father provided through the work of the Son, in the power of the Holy Spirit. Your job is to believe truth and reject lies. Do not throw away your treasure to a con artist or leave it open to be eaten and soiled by rodents.

The Same Old Bag of Tricks

Another way to understand the adversary's schemes is to look at his original strategy in the Garden. Since the time of Adam and Eve, the deceiver has employed the same general pillaging formula found in Gen. 3:1-6: "You will not surely die...for God knows that when you eat of it your eyes will be opened, and you will be like God, knowing good and evil." Notice three deceptive ingredients in this formula:

1. God does not tell the truth (God is holding out on you).

2. You lack what you need (there are hidden things that you do not even know about).

3. It is up to you to obtain what you lack (God will not help so you are responsible for yourself).

Satan constantly uses this template: you cannot trust God; you are lacking something; it is up to you to make up for what is lacking. All his schemes touch on some form of this basic strategy, fearfully driving you toward instant gratification, public adoration, and power through wealth (each without God's help). The following are a few variations on this one theme.

You Are Deficient

The enemy wants to focus your attention on what you do *not* have, while God wants you to consider what you *do* have. If the evil one can get you to fixate on what you lack, you take your eyes off God's good provision. When you choose thankfulness you neutralize the temptation to be a victim. Instead of complaining and whining, learn to be content in all situations, whether facing plenty or want (Phil. 4:11-13). It takes discipline to resist thoughts of deficiency, which is why thankfulness is a primary resource in spiritual warfare (Eph. 5:20).

One type of deficiency is called Fear of Missing Out (FOMO). Perhaps Eve feared being left out of some inner circle, believing that God had a secret knowledge He was holding back from her. The devil got her to believe that if she ate the fruit, she would be on the inside and not left out. The tragedy was, she was already on the inside and gained nothing through her rebellion. In fact, she lost stuff in the deal.

The Answers are Inside You

From birth Americans are conditioned to draw a circle around their personal preferences, evaluating every event as it relates to self. Satan can take advantage of this self-orientation so that you miniaturize your ambassadorship to "my personal relationship with Jesus," where everything is about "me and God." The Bible is reduced to "my personal handbook for living" and the local church is there to "meet my needs." God exists to provide a "wonderful plan for my life." God is there to help you find solutions to your problems by searching inside your personal experience.

Gordon Fee put it this way: "Both secular psychology and much Christian teaching focus on the inner self: How am I doing according to some set of criteria for wholeness? Instead of living out the fruit of the Spirit, in constant thankfulness for what the Spirit is doing in our lives and in the lives of others, our individualistic faith turns sourly narcissistic - aware of our personal failures before God, frustrated at our imperfections, feigning the love, joy, peace, and gentleness we wish were real. In such spiritual malaise God almost always gets the blame."[23]

There is another way to think about the Christian life (see Appendix 7). God's work among His creation is to win back all that was lost at the Fall, and His intent, from the foundation of the world, was to do so through Jesus. He is always working to put all things under Jesus' feet, using the Church to continue the plan Jesus inaugurated. These big issues of life include us, but we are not at the center. The answers to all the cosmic questions in life cannot be found inside you, they are only understood in light of Christ and His Kingdom.

Temporary Amnesia

The adversary wants you to forget who you are, even if it is just for a split second. Simba (*The Lion King*) forgot he was the future king. Neo (*The Matrix*) became confused about who he really was. The Prodigal Son (Luke 15) lost track of his identity and found himself eating from a pig trough. Pinocchio got sidetracked from his quest and wandered to Pleasure Island.

You fight temporary amnesia by putting on the armor of God (Eph. 6). Like Superman, Batman, Wonder Woman, or Spiderman, you put on your clothes to live into your real identity. Knowing that true identity allows you to live according to it, making you less prone to sin and foolishness. You can focus on your duty, your contribution to His Kingdom.

Your Past Dictates Your Future

Satan wants to define your identity, allowing him to frame the debate on his terms. In the movie *The Matrix*, the enemy agent interrogates Neo by slowly leafing through Neo's file. With mocking tones, he refers to Neo by his old name, "Mr. Anderson."

Climbing Up

This is what the adversary does to you. He opens a big dossier, slowly leafing through your past, pointing out your failures. He tries to corner you, framing the debate about your shortcomings, sins, and folly. His interrogation may feel calm, portraying the past in a cool, rational, objective manner. But regardless of how the argument is framed, it is still intended to steal, kill, and destroy. There is a reason he is called the Accuser (Rev. 12:10).

The truth is that you are NOT defined by your portfolio. Nothing in your past or present needs to define you: not your job, not your reputation, not your sins, not your mistakes, not the actions of others, not your sex, not your age, not your race, not your health. God can use you despite your past. He used Moses, despite being a murdering fugitive, and He used Paul, even though he persecuted the Church. Your identity is not defined by the accuser reading your file!

Relax, Take a Day Off

One of the schemes Satan uses is suggesting you take a day off from the battle. One way he does this is by convincing you that the battle is temporary, that it can go away. But the moment you said "yes" to Christ, the fight began. You cannot stop it, and you cannot hope it will go away for a while. Every day you wake up to an onslaught of ideas that rush at you like wild animals.[24] You can never take a day off.

Another way the deceiver urges you to relax is to think that all the important events of life only come in the future. So you let down our guard, thinking the "big game" is coming later. Like Luke Skywalker (in *Star Wars*, who was always looking to the horizon), you can miss the opportunities right in front of you.

Alicia Chole said, "We have a tendency to assume that main thing is somewhere out there, not right here. So we treat today with less respect than we should, as though the current gift of time before us is simply a filler. In such an atmosphere, it is easy for us to rationalize indulging our appetites because, today does not really count, or, we will deal with the issue later, or, it will not make a difference now anyway. All of which are blatant untruths. Today always counts."[25]

It Is Not That Bad

When we sin, we often attempt to justify our behavior. We slander someone, but say, "At least I didn't start the rumor." We dwell on lustful thoughts but are comforted that we are not actually committing adultery. We entertain hateful resentment toward someone but think, "At least I am not punching the person with my fists." We have an amazing capacity to discount our own sin and look down on others who seem more sinful by comparison.

You are most vulnerable to danger when you discount sins because "everyone does it" or because "I am only human." This gives the enemy an opportunity to keep you from confessing your sins and receiving forgiveness. It also allows you to be blinded with spiritual pride and makes you vulnerable to temptations.

Conclusion

In all of Satan's schemes, his purpose is the same: tempt you to voluntarily squander the benefits Christ gave you, to abandon your true identity. The deceiver will employ anything to keep you from focusing on Jesus: distrust God, take it upon yourself to obtain what you need, or practice self-destruction.

Climbing Up

Questions for Reflection

1. Of the comparisons to con artists and rats, which is the most helpful as you reflect on the enemy's deceptions in your life? Why?

2. In what ways have you voluntarily given up the blessings of your identity in Christ, based on the devil's schemes.

3. Put the six schemes of the devil in order of most effectively used to deceive you.

Chapter 13
Playing Your Part

On one side God <u>provides</u>, on the other side the enemy tries to <u>pillage</u>. In the middle, you <u>participate</u> depending on whether you believe God's truth or the devil's lies.

God provides: He desires to produce a return on His investment, overflowing in blessing and abundance for others. His math is based on <u>multiplication</u>. The enemy pillages: He longs to dispossess you, discourage you, and tempt you to self-destructive behavior. His math is based on <u>subtraction</u>.

God's provision is given so He can unleash your potential against the evil one. He is looking to invest in daring people with daring plans, those who are willing to go where darkness reigns; people who are more afraid of missed opportunities than failure.

But most of the time we do not want daring adventures. We prefer stability and clarity. We resist a life of upheaval and disorientation. We find uncertainty frustrating. We want to know where we are going so we can exercise control over our lives. In fact, much of our prayers and efforts are focused on how to control our circumstances, to assure physical safety, financial well-being, and happiness for ourselves and our loved ones. But instead of trying to <u>control our circumstances</u>, our part is to put more effort into <u>taking control of our thinking</u>.

For example, if you live in the country and you leave your front door open, it will not be long before an unwelcomed critter will be in your house. Once it gets in, it may cause damage and will be difficult to remove. In the same way, if you leave the door of your mind open for any stray thought to come in, it will cause considerable damage before you cry out to God to help you get the critter out. The better strategy is to take aggressive control of your thoughts, never allowing the pests to invade your mind in the first place.

Paul's Explanation

Paul says there we can play our part in spiritual warfare in one of two ways: 1) controlling our circumstances "by the flesh" or 2) taking control of our thoughts with weapons having divine power. "For the weapons of our warfare are not of the flesh but have divine power to destroy strongholds" (2 Cor. 10:4).

Dealing with life "by the flesh" is evident when we live as though everything is on our shoulders, believing we must be in control all the time. We act in our own strength, as if there were no God. We attempt to make life turn out the way we want, rather than simply doing what is right and trusting God with the results. We frantically manage our circumstances with gritted teeth and selfish determination.

And living by the flesh is easy to spot because it is full of desperation, anxiety, and disorder. It is constantly scrambling and never at peace. Modern-day America is the most worry-prone culture in history. With 200 classified forms of mental illness, Americans attempt to compensate for their fears with shopping, work, food, recreation, video games, drugs, achievements, and other addictions.

The weapons of the flesh are too weak to conquer the problems of life. We need weapons that have supernatural, divine power. We can pursue inner calm and poise by controlling our outward circumstances (by the flesh), or we can find inner calm and poise through inward conditioning (cooperating with the Spirit to forge our identity). We are no longer debtors to the flesh, but we now live according to the Spirit's forging power (Rom. 8:1-12).

Thanks be to God! He has a different strategy, providing weapons that really work. He forges you into the identity of Christ by making you strong on the inside, like our Lord Jesus. God does this by demolishing the strongholds that have built up in your brain over time from the lies you have believed from the devil.

How Strongholds Form

When ideas come at you (even as you read the words on the page before you), neurons form in your brain. It has been estimated that you have as many as 30,000 thoughts per day. These neurons cluster into branches called dendrites. If you continue to reinforce these branches, after a few weeks of sustained belief, they grow and become hardened into habits and attitudes.

What starts as a seemingly harmless lie, can grow into a permanent stronghold if you let it. Whatever is believed over several days becomes physiologically established in your brain. For example, the enemy may tell you, "You're not a Christian, look at what you just did!" If you accept that lie, believing that God has rejected you, a physical DNA structure forms in your brain at that very moment. Upon several encounters of believing that same lie, it becomes a hardened branch in your brain.

After a few months of accepting this lie, the stronghold becomes so automatic that you do not even think about it. Jesus said people speak out of the overflow of their heart (Lk. 6:45), so when a stronghold is established, you will probably verbalize it without awareness of the harmful effect it has on those who hear you. Negative talk starts slipping out in your conversation, planting seeds of lies in the brains of those who listen, which then reproduces your poisonous thoughts.

Demolishing Strongholds

Praise God, strongholds can be destroyed and replaced with healthy brain structure, much like the process of forging metal. Forging takes the existing molecules in scrap metal but re-forms their crystalline structure to make something new. In the same way, the Spirit takes who you are and forges you to be more like Christ. You are still you, and you do not lose your individual personality. But you become restructured, re-crystallized, and re-wired to become a unique replica of Jesus Christ.

The Spirit forges you into the image of Christ by pounding out lies and replacing them with truth. You demolish strongholds by rejecting lies and replacing them with truth. You crush the toxic crystal structures in your brain, and form a new, stable structure in its place. This requires regular practice of demolishing old lies and replacing them with His truth.

You demolish strongholds by observing the traffic of your thoughts, and then decide which ones can stay and which ones must be destroyed. Just as lies turn into branches in your brain, so truth can form into new branches, replacing what you used to believe.

Besides demolishing strongholds of the past, you can take thoughts captive in the present. The best defense against a stronghold is to never allow it to take root. So when a toxic lie comes at you, choose to detain it by taking it captive. The toxic invader never has a chance to be established.

To take thoughts captive you must interrogate them, asking, "Is that thought friend or foe?" Sometimes you need to say out loud: "That is a lie and I won't receive it!" Call a thought out of the darkness and force it to come into the light. Identify the lie or give it a name. When Martin Luther was troubled by his thoughts, he said, "I am baptized!!" to remind himself of his identity in Christ.

The Enemy's Spin

Think about what happens when people say devastating things to you: "You will never amount to anything." "Why can't you be more like your brother?" "I don't love you anymore." In that moment, the devil rushes in to whisper his interpretation of those words. He wants to put his spin on the statement. He wants to twist their meaning so he can steal, kill, or destroy.

At that moment, you can: 1) choose to believe Satan's deceptive interpretation, building a destructive stronghold; or 2) Choose God's encouraging interpretation that leads to abundant life by taking the thought captive. You can speak back to the enemy's lies by countering with truth.

For example, someone says:

- "You will never amount to anything." (Your response: "No, I am somebody because the Holy Spirit indwells me and gives me gifts to serve His Body").

- "Why can't you be more like your brother?" (Your response: "I do not need to compare myself to my brother or sister or anyone").

- "I don't love you anymore." (Your response: "This person does not love me, but God loves me and wants to use me to bless others; He is not done with me").

Climbing Up

You are not defined by the accuser's interpretation of events. You are defined by God's truth. Like a security guard at the gate of your mind, you can detain a truck that appears to be carrying suspicious cargo. You can pull the truck aside and investigate its contents before letting it inside the gates. As the sentry of your mind, you can take thoughts captive, refuse them entry, and send them packing.

Defending Against Disobedience in the Future

Just because you demolish strongholds of the past and detain lies of the present, it will not stop the Satan from coming back with lies he successfully used in the past. Our friend Daniel Mackey said he has seen many of his fellow returning citizen brothers experience this after their release: "They have hurts and wounds they didn't even know they had. The deceiver had harpoons in them and they didn't know until they got out. Then when a wife or girlfriend acted up or they felt enormous pressure of some kind, the evil one yanked on those harpoons, and to their surprise, they responded in ungodly ways. They got run over because they did not continue seeking the presence of God, staying prayerful and connected to Him. The enemy came back and surprised them."

Mary Flin says: "The biggest thing I find myself teaching former prisoners is the need to walk through pain. Substances and relationships have been used to push pain back for so long. Now they are clean and sober and going back to the community. But they haven't learned how to experience pain without substances and outside the confines of an institution. The ability to navigate pain is a key aspect of spiritual maturity and essential to living through difficult circumstances. I teach them to 'let it hurt; let it heal.'"

Because enemies will return, you must defend against vanquished foes. You may think you have gained control over some stronghold, only to see it re-appear. The adversary will not give up ground easily and will try win it back. You have to keep taking those thoughts captive when they re-surface.

Consider the example of Jesus' temptation. He was victorious over Satan by taking thoughts captive. He countered toxic lies with life-giving truth. But at the end of Jesus temptation, Lk. 4:13 says, "The devil departed from Jesus until an opportune time." If the evil one would look for a later opportunity to tempt our Lord Jesus, you can expect him to do the same to you. Be ready to defend against future attack.

Conclusion

Holding on to your identity will not be easy. Heb. 12:11 says, "For the moment all discipline seems painful rather than pleasant, but later it yields the peaceful fruit of righteousness to those who have been trained by it." If you are willing to cooperate with God, He will equip you to demolish strongholds of the past, detain thoughts of the present, and defend against repeat attacks in the future.

Questions for Reflection

1. List five lies the enemy has told you that may have developed into habits or strongholds.

2. List five truths from God's Word that counter the five lies Satan uses on you.

3. Why is it important to spend more time and energy controlling your thinking than it is controlling your circumstances?

Chapter 14
Daily Practice to Remember Your Identity

THE STUDY OF EPIGENETICS indicates that if you apply meditation and prayer for 10 minutes a day, using different parts of your brain, you can destroy toxic brain structures and replace them with life-giving truth. This can happen in as few as 21 days (see Dr. Caroline Leaf's book "Switch on Your Brain"[26]). You really can be transformed by the renewing of your mind.

Because of God's design, after three successive rounds of 21 days (63 days), your new thinking kicks in and you start controlling you nonconscious thinking. This means you have broken a stronghold to the point that you can disciple others. In 21 days of sustained work, you can start to see progress, and in 63 days you can grow to the point of reproducing the fruit of your life in those who listen. You will start to automatically live out Eph. 4:29: "Let no corrupting talk come out of your mouths, but only such as is good for building up, as fits the occasion, that it may give grace to those who hear."

There is no single way to live out these principles, and you may have your own ways of seeking the Lord and His transformation. But the following is just one description you may find helpful to remember your identity in Christ on a daily basis, taking only about 10 minutes each day (see Appendix 9 for an example):

1. Pray Subordinately

2. Gather Subjectively

3. Focus Objectively

4. Write Playfully

5. Re-wire Decisively

6. Execute Repetitively

Climbing Up

Pray Subordinately

Although every step of this process should be an opportunity for dialogue with God, Pray Subordinately allows you to subordinate your will to God's will. Ask the Spirit to guide your thinking, leading you into truth. Invite Him to shape you into the image of Christ. Spend a moment considering the grandeur of His Kingdom, and your relatively small role in His giant plan for the ages. This will help you place the size of your problems in proper perspective. Ask God to remind you that all the answers in life are outside of you (i.e. the truth is not found within you).

Gather Subjectively

The next step is to gather an inventory of your feelings, which are important because they show you where your beliefs are hidden. Emotions are like a Geiger counter, revealing toxic beliefs that need to be re-forged and healthy truths that need to be re-affirmed.

Neil Anderson said, "Your emotions are to your soul what your physical feelings are to your body. Nobody in his or her right mind enjoys pain. If you didn't feel pain, you would be in danger of serious injury and infection. If you didn't feel anger, sorrow or joy, your soul would be in trouble. Emotions are God's indicators to let you know what is going on inside."[27]

Throughout the Bible God encourages us to pour out our feelings to Him. He is not shocked to hear our complaints, challenges, joys, and fears. The prophets and psalm writers express the rawest of emotions. As the Author of Scripture, the Spirit's inclusion of these examples demonstrate that He is not only tolerant of our emotions, but encourages us to express our deepest feelings.

Daily Practice to Remember Your Identity

A Biblical Example

One clear example is from Habakkuk, "O Lord, how long shall I cry for help, and you will not hear? Or cry to you 'Violence!' and you will not save? Why do you make me see iniquity, and why do you idly look at wrong? Destruction and violence are before me; strife and contention arise. So the law is paralyzed, and justice never goes forth. For the wicked surround the righteous; so justice goes forth perverted" (Hab. 1:1-4).

By the end of the book, God has taken Habakkuk through a process that led him to see clearly beyond his initial feelings: "Though the fig tree should not blossom, nor fruit be on the vines, the produce of the olive fail and the fields yield no food, the flock be cut off from the fold and there be no herd in the stalls, yet I will rejoice in the Lord; I will take joy in the God of my salvation. God, the Lord, is my strength; He makes my feet like the deer's; He makes me tread on my high places" (Hab. 3:17-19). What begins with shattered emotion, ends with affirmation of truth. God clearly uses our feelings to lead us into truth, to forge His identity in us.

Gather Subjectively is a way to list all the various feelings you are experiencing at that moment. Do not be organized or rational, simply list the various emotions you feel (sad, glad, mad, guilty, or scared). This can be written down or done in your head. For example:

- I am worried about my daughter's grades.

- I am happy about something I just learned.

- I am angry about Jim's offensive remarks.

- I feel guilty for losing my temper with Kevin.

Climbing Up

You do not need to evaluate these feelings, assign meaning to them, or counter them with truth. Just inventory them. Your feelings serve as an indicator of what you believe about the circumstances in your life. They help you evaluate where your mental energy is being applied at that moment. Your feelings are like a metal detector that identifies where your beliefs are buried.

Focus Objectively

Focus Objectively is the opportunity to shift your brain into a different mode, to focus your mind on what is <u>objectively true</u>. This is the part when you step back from your feelings and review the truths that apply to your situation.

This is when you list the truths about your situation, noting the facts like a dispassionate observer. Focus Objectively is where you draw from the fruit of past Bible study, memorization, and meditation. The Spirit will lead you into truth as you have invested in His Word. Here are a few examples:

- His grace is sufficient in my weakness (2 Cor. 12:9).

- If I seek the Kingdom first, everything I need will be provided (Mt. 6:33).

- I have an enemy (1 Pet. 5:8).

- This is God's work, not mine (Mt. 9:38).

- I have everything I need for life and godliness (2 Pet. 1:3).

- People are not my enemies; every problem has a cosmic origin (Eph. 6:12).

- No circumstances are beyond redemption (Rom. 8:37-39).

Daily Practice to Remember Your Identity

When you Focus Objectively, you do not have to analyze your personal history. You do not have to figure out how your beliefs went awry. You do not have to dig into your childhood. All you need to do is affirm the truth. Some thoughts and issues in your life are too deep to figure out. You can say like Catherine of Genoa, "I will not wear myself out seeking beyond what God wants me to know. Instead I will abide in peace with the understanding God has given me. And I will let this occupy my mind."[28]

Write Playfully

Having Gathered Subjectively and Focused Objectively, Write Playfully is the time to reconcile your feelings to the truth. It is difficult to accept the truth when your feelings are so strongly at odds with truth. For example, you say you believe that you are forgiven and that God delights in you, but in your heart, you may feel like you disappoint God and He simply tolerates you. You wish you could believe what the Bible says about His love for you, but instead you feel distant from God.

One way to Write Playfully is to put your Gather Subjectively list on the left side of the paper and the Focus Objectively list on the right side. Write Playfully is the bridge to get you from left to right.

This is where you pray or meditate so you can get from Habakkuk chapter 1 to Habakkuk chapter 3. It is important to work through this step until you have reconciled your feelings with truth. Ask the Spirit to clarify why you have trouble believing what God says is true. Having uncovered your false beliefs, you can then cross-examine them, so lies can be put down. You can interrogate your feelings against His Word.

Climbing Up

Research shows that the best way to reconcile thoughts and feelings is through *writing,* i.e. using an old-fashioned pencil/pen and paper. Your brain chemistry is changed when you physically write your ideas because the vibration of the pencil on paper transforms your DNA. However, your Write Playfully work does not have to be limited to words and sentences (journal-style). You can be creative through sketching, doodling, making diagrams, using color or texture, drawing charts, writing a poem, or composing a song. The method you use for writing is not important.

The purpose is to be playful, going back and forth between what you feel and what you know to be true, until you reconcile the two. You need to wrestle with your feelings until they come to peaceful rest under the authority of truth. Write Playfully is the step that harmonizes the truth with your feelings.

Re-wire Decisively

The next step is to move from analyzing your situation to developing a plan of action. You need to stop thinking, stop being a victim, and start taking aggressive action to control your thoughts. This is the time to be decisive as you re-wire the circuitry of your brain. Ask the Spirit, "What kind of person do you want me to become for your glory?" Then, take personal responsibility to put a strategy into motion.

Develop a short slogan that summarizes the change in thinking God wants you to implement. Here are some sample slogans:

- I do not have to impress anyone

- I am not assigned to fix every problem

- I do not have to participate in toxic drama

- Waiting renews strength

Daily Practice to Remember Your Identity

These slogans have deep meaning, because each one represents significant meditation assembled from the steps of forging: Pray Subordinately, Gather Subjectively, Focus Objectively, Write Playfully. There is much thought concentrated in your short slogan, capturing all the previous steps into one short, easy-to-remember phrase.

If you have trouble coming up with a slogan, go back to Write Playfully and see if there is a central thought or idea you can use as your slogan.

Execute Repetitively

Having developed the slogan, the next step of forging is to execute your plan. You do this by scheduling seven opportunities during the day to stop what you are doing and take 5-10 seconds to remember your slogan. Before you see permanent change in your brain chemistry, research shows that you need seven repetitions per day, for 21 days in a row.

For each of the seven repetitions, take only a few seconds to clear your mind of everything else, and concentrate on the slogan. At first this will be harder than it seems because your mind will be distracted by many other thoughts. But if you take 5-10 seconds to discipline yourself by concentrating on the slogan, remembering all that it represents, the process will become more natural in time.

For example, you could select these seven events to rehearse your slogan: when you brush your teeth, before each meal, when you put your head on your pillow at night, and when you open your eyes each morning. Or select seven other occasions that are easier for you to remember each day.

Climbing Up

In each of the seven cases, stop what you are doing, and focus your mind on the slogan seven times each day. The repeated affirmation of truth is what God uses to forge your identity. It is interesting that Ps. 119:164 says, "Seven times a day I praise you for your righteous rules." Perhaps the psalmist had insight into what science is just now discovering: seven repetitions of truth per day can affect us in significant ways.

Bringing the Process Together

The best way to receive Christlike transformation is to think deeply about His truth using different kinds of thinking, but one at a time. Notice how each step uses a different part of your brain and addresses different aspects of your whole person: Pray Subordinately addresses your will, Gather Subjectively inventories your emotions, Focus Objectively focuses your mind, Write Playfully reconciles your emotions to your mind, Re-wire Decisively initiates a plan, and Execute Repetitively promotes self-control so you can avoid being a victim.

This can be done in 10 minutes a day, although you can go deeper on some days if you desire. This is not in replacement of your other spiritual disciplines but is a way to integrate your Bible study and prayer into the rhythm of your daily life.

Ten minutes a day to transform your mind and forge your identity in Christ. You do not have to be highly educated to do this, and you do not have to muster up will power, trying harder not to sin. This is as simple as believing truth and allowing the Spirit to forge you into a different person at a cellular level. Believe what is true and extinguish what is false.

Daily Practice to Remember Your Identity

When you attempt a process of forging, keep in mind that the real goal is to cooperate with the Spirit to make you more like Jesus, not for you to be healthy, well-adjusted, or provide self-care. So do not develop a formula or method but relate to God personally and intimately. Play your part: He forges, you believe. Do not be rigid or legalistic. Make the process work in a way that is natural for you in relationship with Him.

Some situations are complex, may require professional help, or may even have a biochemical source. The ideas in this book are not intended to discourage counseling or avoid medication. Do not let the enemy accuse you of failure if you obtain professional assistance.

Conclusion to Part II: Remember Your Identity

Our friend James Wilson once said, "The three rules of real estate are location, location, location. In the same way, the three rules of the Christian life are identity, identity, identity." This is so helpful, because if you can remember who you are in Christ, you can thrive in re-entry. The question before you is clear: Will you try to *find* your identity (like the world does), or will you allow God to *forge* your identity?

God set us free to represent Him when we remember who He is, a generous, happy, and imaginative Father, who provides us with everything we need. He gave His only Son so we can tap into Jesus' ability to refresh a hurting and confused world, devastated by the lies of the evil one. In whatever situation you are in, the Spirit can empower you as His Kingdom warrior, producing a return on God's investment. So no matter what culture or setting you are in, *be who you are, where you are.*

Climbing Up

In all of Satan's schemes, his purpose is the same: tempt you to voluntarily squander the benefits Christ gave you, and so abandon your true identity. The deceiver will employ anything to keep you from your identity including getting you to distrust God, to take it upon yourself to obtain what you need, or to practice self-destruction. No one can escape the accuser's intrusions, but these invasive thoughts do not need to take up residency in your mind. You can evict them.

You can take control by believing truth and rejecting lies. By cooperating with God, He will equip you to demolish strongholds of the past, detain thoughts of the present, and defend against repeat attacks in the future. Taking only 10 minutes a day, you can cooperate with the Spirit to <u>remember</u> your identity and be transformed by the renewing of your mind.

In *Climbing Up*, first you learned to recognize the culture differences. Now you discovered how to remember your identity. Next is the third and final fundamental skill you need for re-entry: <u>Adapt to Win</u>.

Questions for Reflection

1. Try the six steps every day for ten days in a row, using the same slogan (see Appendix 9 for two examples). Do not give up when it gets hard after a few days. Keep going for 10 days straight.

2. Report the results of your practice over the last 10 days to a friend. How has it helped you remember your identity?

3. Rank order the six steps from easiest to hardest. Which step was easiest and which one the hardest?

Part III: Adapt to Win

"You may work all week on a game plan and then get four plays into the game and realize the plan's no good—you have to be able to adjust."

**- Bobby Bowden, Former Football Coach,
Florida State University**

Chapter 15
The Adventure Begins

As you anticipate your release from prison, you are prepared to soberly "recognize the culture," and joyfully "remember your identity" in Christ. You are equipped so the culture will not confuse you, nor the world define you. But you still need to master the third skill of Climbing Up: how to adjust your plans. <u>You must adapt to win.</u>

You can make an excellent plan only to see it all go out the window in a heartbeat. If you make elaborate plans, where all the elements are tightly woven together, when one of the elements falls through, the whole plan will collapse like a house of cards. When this happens (and it probably will), you can become so discouraged that you may be tempted to give up.

But there is a way to deal with these surprises in a positive way. You can learn how to modify your plans, making it possible to thrive in civilian life. In warfare, the military has a term called "friction" ("things seldom go according to plan"). So even though God is with you, do not be surprised when friction occurs. You will need to zigzag your way to success.

Your journey into re-entry is an adventure that requires courage and flexibility because unexpected problems are certain to occur along the way. There have been many epic stories we could use to illustrate this concept of <u>Adapt to Win</u>, but we chose the *Lewis and Clark Expedition* because it is both full of helpful applications to the ups and downs of re-entry and also ends in resounding success.[29]

Their story is a classic illustration of danger, suffering, unexpected turns of events, intense resolve, and historic achievement. Each of

Climbing Up

the following chapters tells the chronological story of the Expedition (in bold), followed by commentary to help you apply lessons from their experience to your re-entry journey. Let the adventure begin!

Compelling Context

The Lewis and Clark Expedition came in the context of the most famous real estate deal of all time: *The Louisiana Purchase*. In 1803, France had claim to the Louisiana territory that ran from the Mississippi River (on the east) to what is now Montana (on the west) and sold it to the U.S. for only $15 million. This created a great opportunity for American prosperity under then President Thomas Jefferson.

Ever since settlers arrived in the New World, the dream had been to find a water route to from the Atlantic to the Pacific oceans. But the area between the Mississippi River and the Pacific was a huge expanse of unknown and unmapped territory.

No one knew how wide the area was, what the indigenous people were like, how the terrain looked, what vegetation grew there, or what wildlife existed. Even the Native tribes who lived in various regions did not know how one area connected to another. The Louisiana Purchase opened the door to freely explore a northwest water passage without fear of French resistance. But at the same time, Great Britain was also exploring a commercial waterway to the Pacific from their outposts in Canada to the north. A race was on between two world superpowers, so time was of the essence.

Talented but Imperfect

Meriwether Lewis was President Thomas Jefferson's obvious choice to lead the Expedition. Not only was he the president's loyal Chief of Staff, but Lewis was also an accomplished scientist, sharing Jefferson's passion for plants, animals, geography, languages, and cultures. As a young man, Lewis served in the army where he travelled throughout the west, developing frontier skills.

Enormous amounts of scientific information would have to be recorded about the indigenous people, plants, animals, and geography he would encounter. He would have to learn how to take scientific measurements with which to construct a map, lead a group of men into an unknown territory, and then return safely. It was a huge job with tremendous risks.

And Lewis was not without his weaknesses. Jefferson observed several instances of depression which had also been seen in Meriwether Lewis's father. In addition, critics said Lewis was not well-educated and was too much of a risk-taker. There was no question that he exhibited occasional lapses in judgment, especially when Lewis drank too much alcohol.

However, there were few people with his scientific credentials, coupled with his firm constitution, leadership qualities, knowledge of the western woods, and contact with indigenous cultures. Jefferson confidently delegated the enterprise to him.

****

Climbing Up

It is impossible to appreciate the importance of the Lewis and Clark Expedition without understanding the historical context from which it came. Thomas Jefferson appointed Meriwether Lewis to explore a vast area that was completely unknown, report back on what he discovered, and find a water route to the Pacific Ocean. A clear understanding of this context is what kept Lewis's passion alive in the face of obstacles yet to come.

God has always worked His plans through people motivated by their compelling context. Whether it was Gideon fighting against oppression, Noah building an ark, Moses leading the Exodus, David designing the temple, or Nehemiah re-building the broken wall, each person felt compelled to take on their overwhelming project because of their unsatisfactory situation. Their desire to change their circumstances shaped their call and kept them pushing ahead to overcome obstacles and difficulties.

For the biblical characters, and Meriwether Lewis as well, the historical situation energized them to pursue their vision to completion. The same is true in your life. Your re-entry journey will be fueled by your dreams and ambitions, as well as your past successes and failures. The anguish, pain, joy, and fears that shaped who you are today will motivate you to courageously complete your re-entry expedition.

God Uses Imperfect People

Meriwether Lewis was far from perfect. Yet Jefferson was certain that Lewis was the best person to represent him. In the same way, God calls specific people to carry out His work. He calls people from varied backgrounds, of different ages and occupations, both male and female. Looking at the examples in the Bible, there is no single basic profile. They were old and young, experienced and neophyte, arrogant and unsure, proven leaders and beginners.

They were also imperfect people: Noah got drunk at the end of his mission and Abraham lied to save his life. Moses balked at his assignment and required Aaron to serve as his spokesman. Gideon needed four different confirmations to ease his doubts before he believed God. Samson was undisciplined, controlled by sensuality, and confided in untrustworthy people. David abused his power to murder and commit adultery. Jonah took a ship in the opposite direction from his assigned destination of Nineveh, going as far away as he could get. Peter denied the Lord and Paul killed Christians.

Just about every vice known to mankind is exhibited in the representatives God chooses. Yet despite their imperfections, God worked through them. This should give you hope that He can use you to effectively do His work as well.

God Uses Your Background

All of Lewis's past experiences in frontier life and scientific study made him the perfect person to lead the Expedition. In the same way, God used the background of His servants to equip them for their task.

For example, Moses had world-class leadership training in the court of Pharaoh, and after years learning the geography of the desert, he was ready to lead the Israelites out of slavery through the wilderness, and into the Promised Land. As cupbearer to the king, Nehemiah had access to the king of Persia, and all its resources to rebuild the wall. Paul's training as a Pharisee served him well in debating the Judaizers and other heretical teachers.

Climbing Up

Conclusion

God will use every part of your background to make you effective in your future endeavors for His glory. He was at work in you even when you were unaware of Him. In fact, He may have already put something in your background to prepare you for the task ahead. The adventure began long ago before you even knew Christ.

But now an exciting new chapter is about to begin.

Questions for Reflection

1. Study these biblical characters to see how their context motivated them to carry out their assigned work: Gideon (Judg. 6) and Nehemiah (Neh. 1).

2. Before you can Adapt to Win, you must first understand the context in which you find yourself. Think about your context, your history. Write out a history of your life including the key moments that bring you to where you are today.

3. What is unique to your context that God might use for His glory upon release from prison?

Chapter 16
Preparing for the Journey

IN SPITE OF MERIWETHER Lewis's considerable abilities, passions, interests, loyalties, and skills, he needed to receive additional training before he was ready to lead the Expedition. He went to Philadelphia to receive crash courses in botany, geography, minerals, astronomy, and ethnology from the leading thinkers of the day.

While he was studying, supplies had to be procured, a team assembled, and a timetable predicted. They would be out of supply range for an unknown period of time. Forecasting the amount of provisions was especially difficult when the plant and animal life was unknowable.

If they brought enough ammunition, could they live off the land? What kind of medicine might they need with strange, unknown animals or reptiles lurking about? How many men were needed and with what skills? What type of rifles? How much powder and lead? How many cooking pots? What tools? How much rations could be carried? What scientific instruments and books should they bring? How many fishing hooks? Details! Details!

He was especially concerned about the indigenous people they would encounter. There were many legends about the western native tribes, especially the Sioux. Some speculated they were the lost tribe of Israel or a wandering tribe of Welshman. Such wide speculation created a set of planning questions all its own. How could they establish diplomatic relations if the first tribes they encountered turned out to be hostile? What kind of presents would be welcomed by the tribes about which they knew nothing?

It was an overwhelming task to answer these questions, procure what was needed, all while attending intensive studies in every scientific area known to Americans in 1803. He also needed to design and build a modular iron boat that would be needed exclusively for the rapids on the Columbia River near the Pacific Ocean. There was so much to do and not much time.

Finding a Partner

As Lewis considered all these details, he realized the need for a second officer. Not only could another officer enforce discipline, but if Lewis died, there would be someone in command to bring back the journals and report their discoveries. Lewis immediately thought of his old army commander, William Clark. A tough woodsman accustomed to command, Clark was a good waterman and surveyor, and an excellent map maker.

Where Lewis was shaky, Clark was strong and vice versa. Both were competent for the task, reliable, and effective leaders of men. While divided command almost never works in the military (disagreeing commanders can create confusion in the unit), Lewis believed it would work with Clark.

Although they would share joint command, and overlap in their duties, each would have specific roles. Clark would manage the boat and take map readings. Lewis would walk along the shore to collect data and specimens. Lewis also appointed himself the primary doctor. Equipped with only a few medical supplies, he would have to improvise, using what was available from nature along the way.

Building a Team

The initial plan was to send a party of twelve men from St. Louis in August 1803, spend the winter in the Mandan tribal village (North Dakota), cross the mountains to the Pacific and return to St. Louis before the winter of 1804 set in. But by the time Lewis's education was completed, and a plan in place for leadership, it was clear the Expedition would not be ready to leave by August 1803. They would have to wait another year. This would be the first of many times they would have to revise their plans.

With the command structure in place, Lewis set out to build the rest of the team. He needed twelve healthy military men of good character, who were proficient hunters. The success of the enterprise would depend on a careful selection of capable and compatible the men. A long journey into the wilderness, full of unknowns, would be difficult if the crew were not committed to the vision and each other.

They were leaving connection with the outside world. There would be no more guidance from superiors, no orders, no commissions, no fresh supplies, and no reinforcements. They expected to be gone for two years. Lewis and Clark were given an independent military command the likes of which had never been given before, or since.

Climbing Up

Final Preparations

The team met in St. Louis and took the short ride up the Mississippi River toward the confluence of the Missouri River in St. Charles, where they would begin their Expedition. The power of the Mississippi awed them. It became clear they would need a bigger crew. Much more muscle was needed, and more specific roles assigned. As a result, they doubled the size of the team.

But adding to the crew also meant additional financial approval from the president and ordering more supplies. This was no small task in 1803 when it took weeks for postal communication to occur, and up to eight more weeks to receive shipments from the east.

While they were waiting, various duties were assigned to the men. Some would be given daily hunting duty. Sergeants were given command over various parts of the boat. Privates would handle steering, baggage, compass, sails, oars, or lookout. Others would ward off floating debris, or call out warnings of dangers ahead, such as sandbars or whirlpools.

The team had been stationed in St. Charles for four months and had very little to keep them occupied. They were young men in great physical shape, waiting around to start their adventure, so in their boredom they got into fights, got drunk, and were insubordinate.

Finally, the "Corps of Discovery" left St. Charles with joyful spirits and determined resolve. Lewis said, "Entertaining as I do, the most confident hope of succeeding in a voyage which had formed a darling project of mine for the last ten years, I could but esteem this moment of my departure as among the most happy of my life."

More Adjustments to Plan

Lewis and Clark had made initial assumptions about crew assignments, but once they were out on the river, it was a different story. They immediately experienced conditions that differed from their planning assumptions. They needed to adapt.

With cargo aboard, their keel boat was an ungainly craft, so going upstream was almost impossible. They were resisted by a steady current and a variety of islands, sandbars, and narrow channels. Uprooted trees that had fallen into the river had to be pushed out of the way, not to mention branches and limbs that threatened to poke holes in the boat.

Unless there was a tailwind, they had to push and pull the boat upriver. At times they had to rush from one side of the boat to another to keep it from toppling over. Conditions required everyone aboard to be tough, quick, and alert. Thanks to the exertion of the men, the boat and its contents were saved from overturning on countless occasions.

But once they adjusted to their new conditions, their preparation was complete, and they were on their way. They were beginning to operate as a team.

****

Climbing Up

Every important enterprise requires careful planning and preparation. Despite Lewis's knowledge, he still needed additional training in a broad number of topics. In the same way, you should take advantage of opportunities for training while you are incarcerated. Having a broad spectrum of knowledge will equip you for re-entry, even if you do not see a direct or immediate application to life on the outside.

While receiving his education, Lewis also had to think through all the materials and manpower needed to complete the mission, not knowing what to expect along the way. Imagine exploring a place where you know nothing about the people, the geography, the plants and animals, and having to secure all the right supplies.

Perhaps after he learned about a new subject, he went home that night to revise his plans. Maybe after learning about medicine, he thought, "Oh, I will need more of this kind of herb in our supplies." He probably went through many pieces of paper as he updated his list.

In your re-entry planning, you will have to think through a myriad of details as well. Just like Lewis, you are planning for an unknown journey, and you will need to update your plans as you think of new possibilities. You may take a class and think, "Oh, based on what I learned today, I need to update my plan for finding a job." You need to adapt to win, even in your preparations.

Notice that Lewis's men started to crack under the pressure of boredom. They fought, got drunk, and were insubordinate when they had nothing productive to do. Watch out for the enemy's distractions so this this does not happen to you. While you are down, engage in study, service, work, exercise, and any kind of productive activity to keeps your mind and body active.

Your Team

Lewis knew from the beginning that this venture required a team. Lewis and Clark assigned specific roles to talented people, and each person made a unique contribution to the overall enterprise. The same is true of your re-entry. You cannot do this alone. An essential part of your planning involves selecting a team of people to help you. You will do best if you have people helping you *before and after* your release.

Look for a team of people with diverse talents and experiences to give you support and encouragement. Look for people who are strong where you are weak. Believe that God will provide you with people who are led by the Spirit and share your Kingdom perspective. They will help you navigate the culture and remind you of your identity. But you also need specialized experts like your parole officer, who may not be concerned about your spiritual welfare, but can provide much-needed support.

Remember that your team also includes fellow prisoners, the Body of Christ on the inside. Get good counsel from them. Ask them to pray for you. Benefit from the spiritual gifts they provide. They can help you prepare for your release.

In some cases, you might be able to line up some of your team while in prison, but in other cases you will have to wait until you get out. But even now you can start praying for the Lord to provide the right team members to help you when the time comes.

Climbing Up

Adjust Out of the Gate

As important as the planning process was for Lewis, he had to revise his plans based on unforeseen challenges. The discipline of planning is vital, but one thing is sure about plans: they become outdated as soon as they are written. In other words, as you plan you must remember the concept of friction: things seldom go according to plan. No sooner had the Corps of Discovery left St. Charles that they were forced to adjust based on the conditions they found on the Missouri River.

Quentin Valdois reports a common malady that befalls prisoners upon release. They invest considerable time developing elaborate and specific plans in prison. But they set themselves up for failure when these plans are based on fictionalized assumptions about the outside world, underestimated time to accomplish their objectives, and an idealized ability to achieve them. They think about their plans for so long that they become set in stone, and rarely is there a contingency plan to deal with unforeseen changes.

Therefore, you must anticipate that your plans will have to be adjusted right as you leave the prison gate. If you expect this to happen, you can fight off discouragement, saying, "Well, I knew something like this would happen. Adapt to win!"

Conclusion

Make realistic plans during your incarceration, then anticipate successful navigation of the initial surprises you will inevitably face upon release. This will get you started in your ability to adapt to win.

Questions for Reflection

1. Study how these biblical characters conducted careful planning for the assignments God gave them: Nehemiah (Neh. 2) and David (1 Chron. 28).

2. What would have happened if Lewis did no planning and just launched out on the Expedition, confident everything would work out?

3. Why is it important for you to make detailed plans now, even though you know that some things will change later?

Chapter 17
Danger and Disappointment

By July, the Expedition was entering new terrain, rejoicing at the sight of an open, extensive prairie. The beauty of the grass, hills, and valleys was overwhelming. They were excited to start cataloging new animals and plants, unseen in the east, including prairie dogs, buffalo, and jackrabbits. But they were starting to experience danger as well.

Every day, Lewis could be seen making observations in his journal, carrying his rifle and trusty espontoon (a combination sword and rod that could be used to mount his rifle for stable shooting). One day, as Lewis walked along the steep cliffs, he slipped and was headed toward a 300-foot fall into the river below. Just as he was about to go down, he thrust his knife into the hillside and pulled himself up to safety.

Not long after that, Private Shannon failed to come back after hunting. Colter was sent out to look, and when he did not return, a third man was sent. Shannon was not the best of hunters, so they feared he was starving and in a panic. They finally found him after a 16-day chase, 12 of which Shannon had been hunting small animals with pointed sticks and surviving on fruit and berries.

In August Moses Reed deserted the party. When he was found, he was tried in a court martial and found guilty. Meanwhile, one of the key leaders, Sergeant Floyd, had grown grew increasingly ill. By August 20, he died from what appears to have been an infected appendix. They buried him at a beautiful bluff along the river and named it Floyd's Bluff in his honor.

Climbing Up

A few months later another man was also court martialed for insubordination. But the group that remained was loyal and determined to complete their mission.

Concern about Native Tribes

From the beginning, Lewis and Clark were concerned about the unprecedented arsenal of weapons in their possession. In a rendezvous with the Omaha tribe, they were warned that the Teton Sioux, waiting upriver, were intent to kill the Corps of Discovery, take their weapons, and become the dominant force in the region. But Lewis hoped their encounters would be peaceful, talking about trade rather than violent confrontations. Lewis did not want a fight, but he made sure they were never caught by surprise.

In September, the Corps of Discovery met the dreaded Teton Sioux. Lewis and Clark indicated their intention to come as friends and the two cultures cautiously exchanged gifts and speeches. The captains invited the Sioux leaders onto the boat for some whiskey, but then the guests refused to leave. As the chiefs were forced onto a canoe, two warriors grabbed the boat's bowline.

Clark drew his sword and ordered the men to arms. The cannon was swung around. Warriors strung their bows and aimed their guns. It was a dramatic moment. The Expedition was outnumbered. Lewis held the lighted taper over the gun, ready for combat. Finally, one of the chiefs stepped forward to avert hostility.

Danger and Disappointment

Peace had been restored but they had not made a favorable impression. They barely managed to avoid a disastrous exchange, raising concern about their return trip home.

****

Danger can emerge from anywhere, but you can be prepared for it. Lewis almost slipped to his death, but quickly recovered because he was prepared with his knife to stop the fall. In the same way, you can adapt to win by thinking through the dangers ahead and preparing yourself before you get there. For example, if you are going to an old friend's house, have an escape plan in place in the event of trouble. Do not wait for a situation to be right in front of you when you can avoid a parole violation or a sexual temptation.

You can also be prepared by developing a realistic view of life, where you anticipate events to go wrong. For example, if you leave your car at a repair shop, consider the possibility that the repairs will take longer than they tell you and cost more than you originally thought. And when you drive the car home, you may find that they did not fix the problem. By anticipating these possibilities, you do not have to fly into a rage when they occur. Instead you can be proactive by calling ahead before picking up the car, asking for an estimate before they do the work, and ask what to do if the problem persists after driving it home.[30]

When Shannon was lost in the wilderness, he improvised to stay alive by eating plants and hunting without ammunition. When you get into an unforeseen or dangerous situation, look around for a way of escape (1 Cor. 10:13). God will provide, but you may have to

Climbing Up

use your imagination. When you get in a bind, ask God to show you what might be available right in front of you. For example, having a cell phone gives you access to information and people, so use the phone to think creatively about the situation using the tools already available in that phone.

Disappointment

Lewis and Clark also experienced the disappointment of desertion and insubordination from what they thought was a loyal crew. In your re-entry journey, you may find team members who disappoint you, or turn on you. They might argue with each other and put you in the middle. It is disappointing when pain comes from those who were once committed to you.

In war, when soldiers die at the hands of their own comrades, it is called "friendly fire." Sometimes friendly fire takes place in the Church when people criticize, create dissension, fall into sinful behaviors, or simply have a difference of opinion.

Another disappointment occurred when one of the best leaders from the Corps of Discovery died suddenly without knowing the cause. You may lose a team member to illness, death, or simply a significant change in their life situation. As you turn to God for help, be thankful for the loyal teammates who remain, and look forward to God's help as you adapt to win.

Lastly, Lewis knew the likelihood of facing hostile tribes. In the same way, you should not be surprised when you encounter opposition from people. You need to live in peace as much as you can with everyone (Rom. 12:18). Also, although people may cause you difficulty for any number of reasons, your real adversary is the devil and the spiritual forces of evil in the heavenly realms. Remember, you do not battle against flesh and blood (Eph. 6:12).

Conclusion

Danger and disappointment will be part of your re-entry adventure. Do not be surprised by them, but instead prepare for them as much as possible, remembering that God is with you.

Questions for Reflection

1. Study these biblical characters to see how people messed up their plans and dreams: Joseph (Gen. 39) and Nehemiah (Neh. 3-4).

2. List three times when you have made a good plan, with good intentions, and someone (or some event) thwarted your efforts.

3. In the examples from #2, how might God have been at work, even in your disappointment?

Chapter 18
Setbacks and Suffering

By October, the party met the Mandans with whom they were invited to spend the winter. To prevent problems related to idleness, the men were kept busy building a fort, repairing equipment, crafting canoes, hunting for food, and trading with the Mandans. Despite the long winter, and considerable time spent indoors, morale and discipline problems were few.

Without the Mandans' food and hospitality, the Corps of Discovery would not have survived the winter. The men also gained important medical knowledge from the Natives, including a remedy for snake bites, which was later incorporated into the body of Western medicine.

The captains met a French trader named Charbonneau and hired him as an interpreter. He had married a Shoshone woman named Sacagawea who had been kidnaped and sold into slavery to the Mandans. The Shoshones were indigenous to the mountains linking the Missouri and Columbia Rivers to the west, so it would be important to forge a friendly relationship with them.

The captains were unimpressed with Charbonneau but held Sacagawea in high regard. In February, she gave birth to a boy (nicknamed "Pomp" by the crew), with Lewis serving as the midwife. The Corps of Discovery now included not only a full crew of grown men, but a Native American woman and a newborn baby.

Climbing Up

Unknown Territory

Lewis inquired about the next leg of the trip, which was unknown territory. No one had actually made the trip over the mountains to the Pacific, but from what Lewis could patch together there was some clarity about what was to come next.

About 375 miles ahead was a fine, open plain leading to the Great Falls of Montana. After that, the river would split into three forks, then a navigable route to the foot of high mountains dividing the Atlantic and Pacific Oceans. This range of mountains was believed to be crossable on foot in one day, to a river on the west side.

This was exciting news. The vision of finding an easy water passage from the Atlantic to the Pacific was about to be realized. Lewis would be able to send a favorable report to Jefferson that the route to the Pacific was being mapped. This would be the first systematic survey of the area west of the Mississippi, a valuable contribution to the world's knowledge. Spirits were high and the party was eager for winter to end so they could get on their way.

On April 7, 1805, the Corps of Discovery left the Mandan village, ready to set out into new, uncharted terrain. They were ready to explore this new frontier, even though they were unaware of the good or evil they might face. Although they had very few provisions, they were excited because it was the moment they had been waiting for since joining the Expedition.

Problems

After only a few days out from the Mandan Village, a new and unsettling sight appeared: the absence of timber from the landscape. This created a practical problem. The party needed wood to fuel their campfires, and they needed pitch to assemble the modular river boat for their journey down the Columbia. Food was also scarce. But Sacagawea, carrying her newborn baby, was useful in finding wild artichokes and roots that kept the men alive.

Strong head winds slowed them down and even forced the party to stay in camp a whole day. They used the time to dry out damp articles, make repairs to shoes and clothes, and add to the meat supply. The captains caught up on their journaling and made celestial observations.

Grizzly bears had also become a danger. One day, four men fired their rifles at a bear, with two guns held in reserve (back then it took about two minutes to reload and prepare to fire again). The bear rose with a roar and launched a counterattack. The two reserves fired, slowing the bear only for an instant. The men took flight, some to the boats, and others into hiding.

The bear was shot several more times but that only helped the bear know where to chase the men. Two men abandoned their rifles and dove into river. The bear jumped in and was about to reach them when another shot was fired and that finally killed it. Upon examination, it had taken took eight bullets to kill the bear, resulting in a deep respect for the grizzly bear.

Climbing Up

One day, Charbonneau was at the helm of the boat when a sudden squall almost overturned the boat. When he panicked, the boat filled up to within an inch of sinking. From the shore, Lewis watched in horror as precious cargo, journals, maps, instruments, and supplies started to drift away. He wrote in his journal, "If they had been lost, I should have valued my life but little." Meanwhile, Sacagawea, calm and collected, waded through the water to gather up the articles before they became out of reach.

Suffering

Their progress slowed significantly because of frequent bends in the river, head-on winds, shallow water, and protruding rocks. The men had to pull the boats by hand. The water was cold on their legs, the sun hot on their backs. Their footing was either slippery and muddy, or the rocks cut and bruised their feet. Walking on shore was difficult because of prickly pears and cactus thorns which easily penetrated their thick moccasins.

The nights were cold, rainy, and miserable. They often slept in watery beds. The mosquitoes were the worst plague of all, getting in their teeth, ears, and mouths. Even Lewis's Newfoundland dog, who accompanied the party, howled all night from the constant swarm of mosquitoes.

If they had not endured enough suffering, Lewis got dysentery and could not proceed for a few days until a strong medication (which he learned about during his Philadelphia studies) eventually brought relief.

****

When the Expedition wintered with the Mandans, they could not make any progress toward their destination, but they tried to make the most of the situation. What appeared at first to be wasted time turned out to be quite helpful to their overall mission. During their winter's inactivity they made repairs, caught up on journaling, and gathered vital intelligence about the journey ahead. Most importantly, they added a valuable member to the crew, Sacagawea.

In the same way, God can take what seem like losses, and use them for His purposes. Your time while being down might feel like a waste of time. But God can use it to equip, strengthen, and perfect you for His service on the outside. You should take advantage of every opportunity He provides during your incarceration.

Upon release, you may also face setback that seem like wasted time. But God may be at work to provide additional resources for your re-entry, give you time to develop godly character, train you for the future, or deepen relationships.

New Experiences

As soon as the Corps of Discovery was on the road, they immediately experienced new problems. The sight of a treeless prairie was unsettling to them. All their experience had been in frontier situations where trees were plentiful. The joke in those times was that a squirrel could jump from tree to tree from the Atlantic to the Mississippi without touching the ground.[31]

In your journey, you will face situations like theirs, where you have no experience to draw upon and no point of reference. This is why you need people on your team who are familiar with the culture and environment who can help you adapt to win. They survived because

Climbing Up

Sacagawea, who was familiar with that part of the country, knew how to deal with many situations.

Greater Firepower

Encountering grizzly bears was a danger they had not previously experienced. They found out that it took a lot more firepower to deal with this adversary than with anything they had met before. In the same way, you may find new temptations of the enemy in the free world that require significant prayer and more resistance than anything you may have experienced in prison. More than ever, you will need to draw upon the skill to resist the devil (Js. 4:7) from Part II (Remember Your Identity).

Do Not Be Surprised

The Corps of Discovery experienced many kinds of suffering along the way. In the military, these difficulties are called "privation." Napoleon Bonaparte said, "The most important qualification of a soldier is fortitude under fatigue and privation. Courage is only second; hardship, poverty and want are the best school for a soldier."[32]

Do not be surprised when you suffer difficulties upon your release. Peter said, "Do not be surprised at the painful trial you are suffering as though something strange were happening to you. But rejoice that you participate in the sufferings of Christ, so that you may be overjoyed when His glory is revealed" (1 Pet.4:12-13).

God has not abandoned you. In fact, suffering is the *normal* Christian life. Jesus reminded us that we will face tribulation, but that He has overcome the world (Jn. 16:33). Paul desired to share in the fellowship of His suffering, becoming more like Jesus (Phil. 3:10).

James reminds us to rejoice even as we face trials of various kinds because they develop perseverance and maturity (Js. 1:2-4). You can be grateful when things go wrong because it helps you break out of a distorted view of reality that is common in C_p culture (remember Chapter 3).

Conclusion

In your re-entry, you can adapt to win by persevering through trials, bouncing back from adversity, resisting the devil, and staying true to your identity in Christ. No matter what the circumstances, God is at work through setbacks and suffering.

Questions for Reflection

1. Read these passages and consider how people experienced setbacks and suffering: Heb. 11 and 2 Cor. 11:23-27.

2. List three times where you suffered what seemed like a wasted setback and consider how God may have turned it into an opportunity.

3. Read Appendices 1- 2 about testimonies and tips from former prisoners. What are some circumstances where you might face setbacks or suffering in your re-entry?

Chapter 19
Decisive Action

ON JUNE 2, THE party pulled over to the shore of the Missouri River. Across the water they saw two considerable rivers flowing into the Missouri. The Mandans, whose information had been accurate so far, said nothing about this confluence of two rivers. Which of the two rivers was the real Missouri? The north fork or the south fork? Lewis was astonished that such an important item was omitted from the Mandan's report.

The Fork in the Road

This crisis forced the captains to make a difficult decision. Jefferson's orders were explicit: "The object of your mission is to the explore the Missouri River." So, making the right decision was critical to the venture. They were at the proverbial fork in the road.

The north fork was deeper. It ran in the same boiling and rolling manner which had uniformly characterized the Missouri so far. Its waters were of a whitish-brown color, just like the Missouri. The north fork was so precisely like that of the Missouri that the whole party (with two exceptions) firmly believed it was the way to go. The two lone exceptions were Captains Lewis and Clark. Each side was equally firm in their belief.

The south fork was perfectly transparent, had a smooth surface, and ran swifter than the north fork. Lewis reasoned the north fork had run an immense distance through the plains to pick up enough sediment to make it so cloudy, leading him to conclude that the south fork must have come directly out of the mountains. Despite their confidence, Lewis and Clark decided to split up and explore each river to find more evidence.

Climbing Up

After their short excursions, the two groups rejoined. The men continued to believe the north fork was the real Missouri. The captains tried once more to convince the men that the south fork was correct, but without success. But when it came time for a decision, the men wholeheartedly submitted to their captains and proceeded up the south fork (which turned out to be right).

The Difficult Portage

When they reached the Great Falls of the Missouri River, they were surprised to find <u>five sets of rapids with deep ravines</u>, which meant they would be forced to carry everything on land (aka portage). The Mandans had told them there would be only <u>two rapids over a smooth terrain</u>. The 16-mile portage through rough terrain was going to be much more difficult than they imagined. This was the second erroneous report from the Mandans.

The men had to pull with all their might, with wheels catching on stones and grass, while the cactus and prickly pears stabbed them. They were assaulted by hail as big as apples, ferocious mosquitoes, hot sun, ferocious wind, and cold rain. Bears came close to camp at night. They grew faint and their feet were sore.

Meanwhile, Lewis was getting anxious. His plan had been to reach the Pacific and return to winter with the Mandans, but they were not keeping pace to reach the mountains in time. And he desperately needed horses to cross the mountains, which depended on a friendly trade with the Shoshones. As the days went on, with no Shoshones in sight, he became more worried. And even if they appeared, he was not sure if they would be hostile.

Although they were entering the most dangerous part of the voyage, there was no complaining, only resolution and determination. They would succeed or die in the attempt.

****

Lewis and Clark wisely listened to the advice of the entire team before making a decision to take the south fork. And even though time was of the essence, they still took time to explore the options instead of rushing ahead. But when it came time to decide, even though every member disagreed with their decision, the crew was ready to carry out their leaders' best judgment.

You may be in a job or a church where your leaders make a decision with which you disagree. We are not talking about a leadership decision that is unbiblical or that requires you to disobey God, but a directive where you simply disagree. This becomes an issue of *submission to authority*. You need to make it easy for your leaders to lead you (Heb. 13:17, Eph. 6:5-8), even when you do not agree. Submitting to authority is one method God uses to forge us into the image of Christ.

The captains could have blamed the Mandans for giving them bad information about the geography of the Great Falls, but blaming would not get them out of their situation. They were stuck in Montana, with time running out to get over the mountains by winter, but they pressed on toward the goal.

Climbing Up

Likewise, if you get bad information, do not blame or become a victim. Do not let the challenge stop you from moving ahead. Do the best you can with the new situation and adapt to win. If you are presented with surprising and unsettling news, do what Lewis and Clark did: assess, decide, and press on. Even if you end up making a bad decision, you can learn from your mistakes. Stand tall and make the best decisions you can, then live with the outcomes.

Conclusion

Decisive action is needed as you adapt to win. At some point you will likely come to a fork in the road where it is unclear which path to take. There may be not be time to wait until the right direction becomes clear. So when you face these situations, ask God for help and step boldly into the path you choose. Then trust Him to work in whatever you decide.

Questions for Reflection

1. How is Nehemiah a good example of someone making difficult decisions (Neh. 5-6)?

2. What are some examples where you have not submitted to authority and it has caused harm to you or others?

3. As you anticipate your re-entry, do you think you will have more difficulty submitting to authority or taking personal responsibility? Why?

Chapter 20
Dead Vision

As THEY COMPLETED THE miserable portage around the Great Falls, Lewis began assembly of his modular iron boat. The Expedition was counting on this specially designed craft to carry bulky items down the rapids of the Columbia, so a lot was at stake.

But construction was difficult. The prairie continued to be without trees, so they had no pitch to attach the skins together and they were forced to experiment with other materials.

After many days of trial and error with beeswax and buffalo tallow the boat was complete and placed in the river. A wind came up, the skins tore, and the boat was destroyed. Without the iron boat, they would have to figure a different way to carry materials down river. This was a huge loss, physically and emotionally.

Growing Tension

By July 12, they completed the long portage and were ready to pick up the pace. Their hope was still to meet the Shoshones, carry the goods over the mountains in one day, then float down the Columbia River on the other side. Whatever was ahead, they believed it could not possibly be worse than what they had already experienced. Nothing was more arduous than the portage around the Great Falls, and nothing more disappointing than abandoning the iron boat. The worst had to be behind them.

After another week without a sign of the Shoshones, Clark set out to find them. The Corps of Discovery was getting

179

desperate. The next day Lewis saw a column of smoke which seemed like a signal of retreat from one Shoshone party to another. They concluded the Shoshones were aware of their presence but were not willing to meet with the Expedition.

Meanwhile, the riverbed was growing narrower and the mountains looming higher. They had to pull their canoes, and their feet often slipped and were cut on the rocks. The going was tough, each day's progress measured in yards instead of miles. The mosquitoes were relentless. Their discouragement deepened.

The river started flowing southeast, so they were now going in the *wrong direction*. The men were weakening under the continual state of exertion. Clark returned from looking for the Shoshone, his feet bleeding and raw from prickly pears. After a day of rest, he was off again to find the elusive Shoshone.

Some Good News

After two weeks, the party was at a breaking point when, at 9 a.m. they happily reached an important and expected landmark, Three Forks. The view was breathtaking.

But by 3 p.m. Clark came back into camp sick and exhausted with a fever and pain in his muscles. The captains were now desperate to contact the Shoshones. Soon they would be in the mountains with a scarce food supply, and without adequate information about the geography. They could wander in the mountains and die. Without Shoshone horses, turning back would be the best option.

On the other hand, the captains remained optimistic, believing if the indigenous tribes could survive the mountains, their men could do the same, so they kept going, hoping each day for good news.

One day Sacagawea informed the Expedition they had reached the spot where the raiding Hidatsa tribe had taken her prisoner five years before. Despite reaching this landmark, they were fatigued and morale was sinking fast. They were forced to abandon another canoe to lighten the load. The men wanted to carry what they could on their backs and leave the rest behind but the captains thought it was unwise. They needed horses, and soon.

Another Concern

There was also growing doubt about the navigability of the Columbia on the other side. Logic indicated the Columbia had a shorter time to descend the mountains, resulting in more waterfalls, and more portages. But the captains remained hopeful. Their approach was to stay positive until events proved otherwise. They believed that when they got up to the mountain top, they would see something similar on the other side.

Lewis decided they would split up, sending a party to find the Columbia and horses, even if it took a month. It was a do-or-die moment. He continued to have unshakable confidence in his ability to find the Shoshones, and then successfully negotiate with them.

Climbing Up

The Shoshones at Last

On August 9, Lewis looked through his telescope and spotted a Native American on horseback, presumably a Shoshone, about two miles ahead and coming toward him. Lewis was overjoyed. He knew if he could get close enough, he could prove his peaceful intent. But when they were about a mile apart, the Native American stopped. Lewis laid out a blanket on the ground as a signal of friendship.

Shields and Drouillard were accompanying Lewis along parallel paths, but out of Lewis's shouting range. Lewis was afraid to alert his party for fear of raising the Native American's suspicions. He sat on his horse until Lewis was within 200 yards and then slowly moved away.

Lewis called in loud voice. Instead of responding to Lewis the rider watched Drouillard and Shields, who were not paying attention to what was happening. When Lewis was within 100 yards the rider suddenly turned his horse about, gave it the whip, leaped the creek, and disappeared in the willows. This destroyed all hopes of obtaining horses.

Lewis was devastated.

Could It Get Worse?

Three days later, Lewis discovered a fountain representing the headwaters of the Missouri. He proceeded to the top of a dividing ridge, looked up to the west, and had the shock of his life: before him was an immense range of high mountains partially covered with snow. It was a full view of the towering

Rocky Mountains, far bigger and more imposing than anything he had seen or could imagine.

With this sudden discovery, it became obvious there would be no one-day portage over low-lying mountains, as reported by the Mandans. The geography of hope gave way to the geography of despair. There was no easy water route over a gentle divide. The vision of finding an all-water route from the Mississippi to the Pacific was now dead. In the matter of seconds, decades of hopes were shattered.

The Expedition was deep in unknown territory, without much left to trade. They had no Shoshone contacts for horses. The scout may have alerted the Shoshones to stay away from the new strangers. The iron boat was destroyed. Clark's group was off to some unknown place looking for the Shoshones. There was no all-water route to the Pacific.

For Meriwether Lewis, the vision was dead.

****

Meriwether Lewis experienced the death of his vision. With the sight of the Rocky Mountains on August 12, 1805, Lewis saw his hopes to find a North American all-water route go down the drain.

You may be surprised to hear that "death of a vision" is actually normal for those who have walked with God, and it is likely to be true in your life too.[33]

Abraham, Joseph, Moses, Esther, all experienced the disappointment of seeing their vision die. God seemed to give them a vision that raised their hopes, only to have them dashed, resulting in the dead vision.

Each of them had hopes and dreams but found themselves in hopeless situations. Abraham was told to kill his only son, who God promised to be Abraham's heir. Joseph expected to be exalted above his brothers but landed in prison with no hope of escape. Moses was set to be Israel's deliverer but fled Egypt as a fugitive and became a shepherd in the desert. Esther was in a hopeless situation as her people were about to be extinguished.

Perhaps the clearest picture of dead vision came on Good Friday, when the disciples watched Jesus die. Only a few hours before, people believed that Jesus was the promised Messiah. The prophets had predicted His coming to save Israel. Even John the Baptist believed that Jesus had come to fulfill the apocalyptic prophecies about the conquering King. When Jesus was crucified and buried, the disciples' vision died, along with Jesus.

Death of Your Vision

The death of your vision can come in many forms. You may lose a friendship; you may lose hope for finding a job; your plans for ministry may evaporate. Family members may abandon you, or sudden illness could come upon you. These are not just trials or setbacks, but full-on game-changers that obliterate your entire understanding of the future.

You may wonder if you really heard from God, or if your vision was just something you made up inside your head. Or you may blame others for setting you up for disappointment. It may seem like all hope is lost and there is no way forward.

Like most of God's people, you will probably experience dead vision at some point in life. When you do, you may be tempted to despair. You may even consider going back to a life that could send you back to prison.

Conclusion

For those who follow Christ by faith, dead vision is the moment of truth. How you handle dead vision makes all the difference. Those who trust God, holding their plans with open hands, can see God at work. God has His ways and time frames that are different than yours.

Questions for Reflection

1. Study characters in the Bible to see how they handled their dead vision: Joseph (Gen. 40) and Esther (Esther 3-4).

2. In your re-entry, what are some ways that you might experience dead vision?

3. What should your response be if you face a dead vision?

Chapter 21
Renewed Vision

ON AUGUST 13, 1805, the very next day after his demoralizing view of the Rockies, Lewis's group stumbled upon three Shoshones—two women and an old man. Lewis exchanged gifts and persuaded them to introduce him to their tribe.

Two miles later they found the sight they had long anticipated—sixty Shoshone warriors on horseback armed for war. As the Shoshones halted the group, Lewis laid down his rifle as a sign of peace. The warriors would have attacked Lewis's party if not for the presence of the three Shoshones accompanying them. The chief approached Lewis and warmly placed his arm around him. They had finally met the Shoshones and received a friendly welcome.

While waiting for Clark's group to arrive, Lewis inquired about the passage to the Pacific. The Shoshones told them about the upcoming mountain pass, which was barely passable, but they had not been down the river, which they heard had rapids so rocky that it was hopeless to pass by land or water. This report made it official: There was no trans-continental trading route, or anything remotely resembling it. Not only was it impossible to carry goods over the pass, it was also out of the question to go by horse along the river.

However, Lewis was encouraged to hear about the Nez Perce tribe who lived on the west side of the Rockies on the river. The Shoshones reported that the river flowed "into a great lake of ill-tasting water toward the setting sun." This apparent reference to the Pacific Ocean connected the continent together and gave them renewed hope.

Climbing Up

For the first time there would be a known geographical link between the oceans. The Shoshones said the Nez Perce crossed the Rockies going east every year to hunt buffalo on the eastern plains. This meant that the Nez Perce would be the only tribe to give them the ideal route connecting the Pacific to Plains. If the Corps of Discovery could work with the Nez Perce to discover this optimum route, part of their mission could be salvaged. They could still fulfill their objective of reporting the best route way to get from the Mississippi River to the Pacific Ocean.

More News

Lewis also learned about the challenges ahead. The passage was difficult and there was no food, so travelers had to go hungry or eat berries to stay alive. But Lewis stayed optimistic: "If others could do it, we can too." Every time they faced a challenge, Lewis always believed that it could not possibly get worse. Despite the discouraging report, the party's motivation was still alive, and Lewis believed the men would rise to the occasion for the sake of the mission.

To proceed, Lewis needed to purchase Shoshone horses and guides to get to the Nez Perce. Since the Shoshones needed guns to hunt buffalo, Lewis offered them future arms and support from the government. Negotiations almost broke down when some of the Shoshones suggested that Lewis was in alliance with their enemies and preparing an ambush. Lewis confronted them strongly, questioning their courage and challenging their manhood. The strategy worked, because the horses and guides were secured, and negotiations completed.

However, Lewis was nervous that Shoshone suspicion might re-occur when part of Clark's party came into camp, fully armed. Wanting to lessen their fears, Lewis gave his rifle to the chief and informed them of a Shoshone woman (Sacagawea) who was in their group. This further inspired their confidence, so Lewis asked one of the warriors to accompany Drouillard to find the rest of the Expedition and bring them back.

When the rest of the group arrived, a commotion broke out. One of the young Shoshone women, Jumping Fish, recognized Sacagawea. Jumping Fish was with Sacagawea the day she was abducted by the Hidatsas. The two women cried and talked all at once for several minutes. Then Sacagawea looked up, saw Chief Cameahwait, and jumped into his arms, sobbing profusely. It was her brother!

No novelist would dare invent such a touching scene.

****

It was less than twenty-four hours after the death of Lewis's vision (seeing the full sight of the Rockies) that his vision was renewed by their friendly meeting with the Shoshones. And if that was not enough, they reconnected Sacagawea with her friends and family, among whom was the chief, Sacagawea's brother!

When God gives a vision to someone, even if it seems to be extinguished, He will resurrect it in His time. He gives a supernatural fulfillment of the original vision, often in unimaginable ways.[34]

Just when Lewis's vision seemed dead, new hope emerged. He gained new realization that there was a way to complete the task

Climbing Up

Jefferson had entrusted to him. Renewed vision often comes after your dreams are dashed. You can expect God to bring fresh hope after a time of despair, so it is important to keep going even when the outlook seems bleak. Renewed vision could be around the next corner.

The Disciples

Jesus' death on the cross was devastating to the disciples. In fear for their lives, they hid in Jerusalem for three days, shattered by the previous days' events. Early Sunday morning, a group of women left for the unhappy task of anointing Jesus' body at the tomb. As they approached, an angel of the Lord appeared to them and said, "Do not be afraid, for I know that you are looking for Jesus, who was crucified. He is not here; He has risen, just as He said" (Mt. 28:5-6).

Their gloom was turned to inexpressible joy. The angel told them to go back and tell the disciples. As they were on their way, they met up with Jesus himself. Hurrying from the tomb, they ran to report this happy news. Their three days of dead vision had been resurrected by Jesus himself.

Adjusting Your Expectations

In your re-entry adventure, you need to trust God if you face dead vision. You may also need to adjust your understanding of how that vision will be carried out. You may have had expectations that your plan would go through steps 1-2-3, but He may take you through steps 3-9-7.

This is why you need to hold your plans loosely so you can adapt to win. Keep the big picture in mind, but revise your plans to get there. For example, we felt a call from God to help former prisoners find their place of Kingdom service upon release. We had specific ideas on how this would happen, thinking it would be through the ministry with which we had served for 30 years. However, through mutual agreement with our leaders, we discovered that our vision was dead.

But God had a different path for us to take. The vision was still the same, but the road that got us there was unforeseen. He led us to start a brand-new organization, even though we were in our late 50s. We left our Los Angeles home and church where we raised our children, and moved across America to a new state, where we had no friends or supporting church. We felt like Abraham and Sarah moving to a place we did not know.

It was a difficult time but we kept moving forward in faith, even when the vision seemed dead. Over the next months, He opened doors and established our ministry even more strongly than we had anticipated! God brought renewed vision and resurrection life to what seemed like dead vision.

Conclusion

Even when it seems that vision is dead, if it is God's will to continue, He will revive it in His time and in His way. God is in the business of renewed vision. He gives resurrection life. He can do the same for you.

Questions for Reflection

1. Study the people who experienced renewed vision and reflect on how God changed their situation in unexpected ways: Abraham (Gen. 22) and Esther (Esther 7-8).

2. Talk to three people about what you learned about dead vision and renewed vision and ask them if they have ever had a similar experience.

3. If you find yourself in the middle of dead vision, how might you adapt to win and prepare for renewed vision?

Chapter 22
Daring Perseverance

WITH THE SNOW-COVERED MOUNTAINS before them, the Shoshone guides to lead them, and the Missouri River behind them, the Expedition started their perilous climb. According to the Shoshones, it would take at least six days to cross.

Before long they were nearly out of food. The route went through thickets on rocky hillsides where the horses were in constant danger of falling. In fact, on several occasions the horses fell to what appeared to be certain death, but to the party's amazement, the horses got up with minimal injury.

September 16 was the worst day of the Expedition to date. Eight inches of snow fell. Clark said he had "never been as cold in every part of my body as I ever was in my life." The horses and men were near starvation, so some of the horses had to be eaten as food.

Spirits were low and the men were approaching their limits of physical endurance. Several of the men were sick with dysentery, yet retreat was unthinkable. They would rather die than quit. Besides, a five-day journey back was impossible. Killing more horses would mean abandoning most of the baggage, so it was decided that Clark should take six hunters ahead to find food.

After six miles, Lewis reached a ridge, and to his inexpressible joy, he saw a large prairie descending to the west. The next day Lewis found food that Clark had left for them, which lifted the men's spirits. With the party's strength renewed, Lewis ordered an eleven-day forced march over 160 miles of rough terrain before reaching the lodges of the Nez Perce.

Meeting New Friends

The Expedition had conquered the Rockies, thanks to outstanding leadership, disciplined perseverance, and the skill of their Shoshone guides. During this ordeal, the Corps of Discovery did not sulk, lash out at their leaders, or insist on retreat. They had formed into a unit committed to the success of the enterprise.

Twisted Hair was chief of the Nez Perce. He told the Expedition they were ten days away from of a set of falls and a few weeks from the ocean. The captains had learned that estimates from the Native tribes could be optimistic (or they were able to travel much faster), so Lewis and Clark listened cautiously to the report.

During their visit with the Nez Perce, several men were sick with complaints of heaviness and bowel problems. They had eaten a boiled root that filled them with so much gas that they could scarcely breathe. For twelve days they continued to be sick, becoming feeble and emaciated, leading them to name the area the "Bitterroot Mountains." In their vulnerable condition, it would have been easy for the Nez Perce to kill them and steal their priceless goods.

But the Corps of Discovery developed a friendship with the hospitable Nez Perce, who asked the captains to stay longer. They were torn between their desire to keep moving and the goal of bringing the Nez Perce into the American sphere of diplomacy. Rather than linger, they decided the crew would stay for a longer visit during their return trip in the spring of 1806.

Risking the Rapids

With the loss of the modular iron boat, the Expedition needed a new way to travel down river. They found a great solution from their new friends the Nez Perce, who were experts in crafting burned-out canoes. When they were finished building canoes, they were off once again, quickly reaching the junction of the Snake and the Columbia Rivers (in present-day Washington).

As they proceeded, they encountered rapids that seemed too dangerous to travel. Their canoes were cumbersome and could easily be swamped, springing leaks on many occasions. The Expedition faced as many as fifteen dangerous rapids per day. Each time, the men pressed the captains to run the rapids rather than waste time making portages. Their Shoshone guide, Old Toby, was so frightened by their daring actions that he left in the night without receiving his pay.

When they reached a set of falls (now known as The Dalles, east of Portland, Oregon), Clark was appalled by the horrid appearance of this "agitated gut-swelling water, boiling and whirling in every direction." In modern terms it was a Class V, meaning even a modern canoe, designed for rapids, could not survive it. The captains removed selected items that would be carried on land such as journals, rifles, and scientific instruments. Then they proceeded to run The Dalles in their canoes.

The native tribes, who were expert canoeists, came by the hundreds to the banks of the river to watch the foolish white men drown themselves. They were also ready to collect the Expedition's equipment and supplies upon their demise. But to the astonishment of the onlookers, the travelers survived without incident. Later, they repeated this feat at Long Narrows, again before a crowd of indigenous spectators watching them defy the odds.

A New Cultural Experience

As they made their way down the Columbia, the Corps of Discovery encountered the Chinook, Tillamook, and Clatsop tribes. These cultures were not as warlike as the Plains tribes, but the Chinooks were constantly stealing from the Expedition. The team's supplies were limited, so any loss was significant.

The men had to be restrained from violence because of their frustration over this series of thefts. The party was not looking forward to a winter with these tribes, after such a warm friendship with the Nez Perce and Mandans.

On November 2, they reached western territory that had been previously mapped by other explorers. Now the maps of east and west could come together for the first time. They were making good progress every day and, on November 7, sighted a large body of water, an inlet to the Pacific Ocean.

****

First, the vision was dead. Then it was renewed. The Corps of Discovery had fought through many grueling physical challenges. The trek through the mountains was difficult beyond description. The men were sick and vulnerable. Only the kindness of the strangers kept them alive. Having crossed the Bitterroot Mountain pass, the Corps of Discovery could have settled down for the winter with their new friends, but they kept going toward their goal.

Daring

Lewis and Clark faced difficult decisions along the river. Would they play it safe and go around the rapids on foot, or was it worth the risk to face Class V rapids in homemade canoes to keep on schedule? To reach the Pacific Ocean before winter, they chose to be bold and run the rapids. Others looked on in disbelief as they conquered the danger.

In your re-entry adventure, you may be called to have the courage to leave the comfort of the safe or familiar. There may be times for you to be daring and take calculated risks. You should not be reckless or impulsive, but sometimes it is right to step out in faith and take courageous action if you are going to adapt to win.

Perseverance

In your journey, after facing many emotional events, one after another, it is tempting to get tired and give up. For the Expedition, there was no turning back, and the same may be true for you. In some situations, you need to simply persevere, to keep on going, keep showing up.

We have lived through many of those moments. Don recalls dozens of days walking up the stairs to go to work in the morning wondering if he would have the stamina to endure the traumatic events of the day before him. As he would pray for strength, many times he sensed the Lord saying, "Just take the next step." In taking that step, the energy Don needed would come back, and his strength renewed. Many times, you simply need to do the next thing and do it well.

Missing Friends

The Expedition also encountered the unpleasant company of thieving tribes along the river. They longed to be back with their friends. The same may be true in your life, wishing you were back with your brothers or sisters in prison, finding it difficult to live among a new culture on the outside. But if you press on, God will provide new friends and new energy.

Conclusion

In your re-entry, there will be times that you need to be take a risk. Pray, assess the situation, then proceed. Perseverance is also important because Satan will continuously try to get you to give up just before breakthrough comes. Daring perseverance is a good phrase to live by.

Questions for Reflection

1. Read about these biblical characters who were willing to leave the safe and comfortable to exercise bold and courageous action under God's guidance: Gideon (Judg. 7) and David (1 Sam. 17).

2. Think about three examples where you were daring and bold, and then three other times where you were reckless and impulsive. How can you tell the difference between Spirit-led boldness and human-centered impulsiveness?

3. Think about your re-entry and consider some situations where you will need to persevere rather than give up.

Chapter 23
Patience and Caution

THE EXPEDITION REACHED A campsite but then they were unable to move forward or retreat due to a rainstorm that trapped them for eleven days. Fires were difficult to start. Their bedding was soggy all night long. Their clothes were nearly rotted away. They looked more like survivors from a shipwreck than the triumphant members of the Corps of Discovery. The wind increased with such violence that it threw immense waves over the banks and overwhelmed the party. Clark said, "O how horrible is the day."

Lewis had not made a journal entry for two months. Historians speculate that he was suffering from the depression that originally concerned Lewis's critics. The rigors of the Columbia's falls reinforced that there was no easy water route across the continent, so it could have been that Lewis was discouraged about the report he had to give Jefferson. Lewis may have also been despondent about the return voyage, knowing how difficult it would be to get back home safely.

Whatever Lewis may have been going through is purely guesswork. But if he did suffer from depression, it was a special mark of heroism that he could lead the project under such conditions. It is even more astounding to consider that he may have been an alcoholic who had gone without liquor for four months. He had quit "cold turkey" to lead the complex and dangerous mission across an unknown frontier.

Despite the silence of his journals, Lewis demonstrated the courage to press on. The journey would be a failure if he could not get the journals back to Jefferson. The water route was important, but the scientific discoveries were now the primary object of his work. He had to get that information back to his boss.

Setting Up Camp

The Expedition needed to find a winter camp, but they were immobilized by the weather. They had to be rescued by the Clatsop tribe, who gave them food and suggested alternative places to set up their winter home. The captains had to choose a location based on three conditions: close to game (for food); near the ocean (to spot a possible passing ship and supplies); a convenient place to refine salt from the ocean.

Typically, the captains made the decisions, but this time they let everyone participate in a vote. Even Sacagawea (a non-citizen woman) and York (a slave) participated. It was the first time in American history that a Native American woman and a Black man were given the right to vote. The group decided on a forested area between the Columbia and the Pacific and called it Fort Clatsop, in honor of their new neighbors.

The Winter of Waiting

The party spent the next few months making salt and new clothes, repairing equipment, and recovering from injuries. Throughout the winter, it rained constantly, and their camp was infested with fleas. The men were constantly ill with fevers and influenza, and the captains were unable to make celestial observations because of the consistent cloud cover. It was difficult to be patient. They were eager to get back on their way.

Clark worked on his map, connecting the previously unknown section from Mandan to Clatsop, providing an invaluable contribution to the world's knowledge. Sacagawea was excited to see the ocean, the first Shoshone to do so. But for the other members of the party, the winter at Clatsop was unbelievably dull. One day the boredom was broken when a whale beached on the shore, providing valuable blubber that the Expedition could use in trade on the way home.

On Christmas morning everyone exchanged presents, such as they were, which only made them more homesick. No ships ever passed by to bring them supplies. Clatsop became more like a prison than a winter home.

As the party prepared to leave Clatsop and head home, the captains received reports that salmon was scarce and tribes were starving upriver. But they could not afford to wait too long and get caught for another winter before reaching St. Louis. So on April 7, 1806, the Corps of Discovery finally set out from Clatsop. Compared to their plentiful supplies at Mandan, they departed with almost nothing.

Frustration Sets In

As they travelled upriver, they continued to be victimized by constant petty theft. Anything left unguarded, even for a moment, was gone. When Lewis's dog was stolen, his pent-up anger turned into full-blown rage. He sent out a team to shoot the thieves, if needed.

The party was at the edge of serious violence. Giving in to their frustration would not only ruin relationships with the people they were trying to befriend, but also put the whole Expedition in danger. When the dog was found, Lewis calmed himself and reconciled with the chief whose tribe had committed the dognapping.

But as they moved on, their troubles were not over. On May 1, the weather was miserable, and the captains divided the last portion of food. There was nothing left to eat. The party was on the brink of starvation.

Rescued by Friends Again

After three days without food, the party encountered a band of Nez Perce who sold them some roots to eat, saving them from starvation. They were rescued from extinction once again.

They were escorted back to Chief Twisted Hair who had kept their horses over the winter. The captains found Twisted Hair in conflict with another tribal chief. Lewis and Clark were able to mediate a peaceful reconciliation, which only strengthened the bonds of trust and friendship between the Nez Perce and Corps of Discovery.

The previous year, Clark had healed an old man's knee, so while they were gone, Clark's reputation as a healer had grown with the Nez Perce. When Clark arrived in the village, he was surprised to be in great demand as a doctor for the people in distress, which proved useful in trading.

The mountains ahead were covered with snow, so the Nez Perce counseled them against making passage until June. Morale sank at this news. This would mean a three-week delay, and they were very eager to keep moving.

To increase morale, athletic contests were held between the Corps of Discovery and the Nez Perce. Spectators from each culture came out to cheer them on. The party enjoyed their time with the tribe and a genuine friendship developed. But the men were tense, ready to vault over the mountains.

Wise Counsel or Unnecessary Delays

The snowfall that year was greater than normal and the Nez Perce warned it could be July before the Expedition could depart. A premature departure could result in forcing the horses to go without food for three days. But the Nez Perce advice did not keep them from setting out. By June 9, the party was elated with the prospect of moving toward home. Just before the Corps of Discovery left, the Nez Perce promised to send guides to catch up with them.

After a few days, the captains were concerned because the Nez Perce guides had not arrived. The captains decided to not to wait. This was a big risk, but Lewis felt the need to keep moving.

Within four hours, they faced harsh winter conditions. They were six days away from safety, assuming they did not get lost along the way. If they did get lost, their horses would die and they would risk losing the journals and instruments that were essential to their mission.

The captains realized the foolishness of their decision and turned back to get guides while the horses were still strong. On June 17, for the first time in the Expedition, they were making a retreat, but for good reason. They sent a small group party to find the Nez Perce while the rest of the party waited for them. On the third day of waiting, the group appeared with the guides.

Safety with Guidance

After a week they reached an elevated spot with an extensive view of the mountains, which filled them with awe and dread. They had made the right decision to get help. The trail was covered with ten feet of snow, heavily wooded, and often dangerous. They developed a deep respect for the Nez Perce guides. It seemed impossible to have escaped without their assistance.

On June 30, they reached camp at a place they called "Traveler's Rest." It was time to say a sad goodbye to their friends. The two cultures had shared experiences that drew them together. The Nez Perce could not hide their anxiety for their new friends, believing the Plains tribes would kill the party before arriving safely home. The Expedition would not have survived without their comrades to feed them when they were hungry, provide fuel when they were cold, outfit them with horses and guides, and offer wise counsel that saved them from perishing.

****

Waiting at Fort Clatsop had become the worst part of the journey. The weather was bad, they had little to do to keep them busy, and they were eager to start back home. But while they were at Clatsop, seeds that were sown with the Nez Perce had come to fruition. Their investment in caring for the sick resulted in a demand for Clark's expertise upon return, which strengthened their economic position and deepened their friendship.

In your re-entry experience, you may face a season of waiting. It may be the most difficult part of your journey, but God is often at work in your waiting. The seeds you plant will take time to grow and take root. He uses times of waiting to accomplish things we cannot see.

The Supremes said, "You can't hurry love, you just have to wait." In the Kingdom, the same can be true—you just have to wait. "They who wait for the LORD shall renew their strength" (Is. 40:31).

God's Work in Man's Way

The Corps of Discovery was frustrated by petty theft. They were tempted to take matters into their own hands, which would have been disastrous.

Abraham demonstrated great patience for twenty-five years, waiting for the promise to be fulfilled. Then he had a lapse in judgment and fathered a child son named Ishmael through Sarah's maidservant, Hagar. Abraham was trying to fulfill God's promises in his own way. Although his motives were right, it was a bad idea that had lasting implications.

Sometimes you will be tempted to take matters into our own hands, to do God's work in your way and your timing. Be careful that you do God's work in God's way.

Ignoring Wise Counsel

Although Lewis and Clark wanted to press ahead, they realized that the Nez Perce were giving wise counsel to wait. It was painful to hear, and at first, they ignored their input. But the captains eventually revised their plans and turned around to wait for guides and better travel conditions.

Climbing Up

In your journey, you should seek wise counsel and listen to it, even when it is hard to hear. "The way of a fool seems right to him, but a wise man listens to advice" (Prov. 12:15). And like Lewis and Clark, if you make the wrong decision, you must be humble enough to turn around and come back.

Conclusion

Patience and caution are needed if you are going to adapt to win. In your re-entry adventure, one of the most significant virtues you need is the ability to stay calm.[35] While boldness is sometimes the right choice, there are other occasions when the wise thing is to wait, be patient, and exercise caution.

Questions for Reflection

1. Study what happened when Esther waited a day before acting (Esther 5-6).

2. List five events in your life where you had to wait. In each of the five examples, did you react by taking matters into your own hands, or were you able to wait patiently, trusting that God was in control?

3. Think about your release. What are some situations where it would be important to seek counsel to revise your plans, even if you are confident about those plans?

Chapter 24
Courage to the End

By June 30, 1806, Lewis and Clark had escaped much of the danger and unknown and were clearly on their way home. For the most part, they had completed their mission, but the captains still had a few more objectives.

They wanted to provide Jefferson with an optimum land route across the continent, explore the northern boundary of the Louisiana purchase, and strike a trade deal with the Blackfeet (whom they had not met on their trip west). So, the captains split the Expedition into sub-parties, according to a plan they had devised during their winter at Clatsop.

On August 11, Lewis and Private Cruzatte went elk hunting in the willows. As Lewis raised his rifle to shoot, he was hit in the rear by a rifle shot, spinning him around. Lewis yelled at Cruzatte but there was no response, so Lewis assumed it was an attack from a Native tribe.

In an effort to rally the men, Lewis ran 100 yards toward the boat and called them to arms. After struggling to get in the boat, he waited in terrible suspense for the rest of the group to return. Finally, after twenty minutes, the crew arrived. When the bullet was removed from Lewis's behind, it was an Army-issue bullet, proving that Cruzatte had shot him by mistake. Lewis ordered the men to move on, their commander lying face down in the boat, in pain and humiliation.

The next day, the groups joyfully met up again, having achieved their objectives, despite Lewis's embarrassing experience.

Climbing Up

Two days later they were back with their friends, the Mandans, who were extremely glad to see the Corps of Discovery alive.

Preparing to Go Home

After a week with at the Mandan village, they compensated Charbonneau for his services, and complimented Sacagawea for her outstanding service. She had accompanied them on a long, dangerous, and fatiguing route to the Pacific Ocean and back, with a newborn baby. The captains said, "She deserved a greater reward for her attention and service on the route than we had in our power to give her."

Clark had become so attached to her baby son, Pomp Jean Baptiste, that Clark offered to adopt him as his own. Years later, Charbonneau sent Pomp to live with Clark to receive an education. As an adult, Pomp traveled through Europe before becoming a western explorer in his own right.

With most of their challenges behind them, the men started thinking more about home. They were starved for news. A presidential election had taken place but they did not know the outcome. The country could be at war with another country for all they knew. They had become real-life Rip Van Winkles.

They visited Sergeant Floyd's grave at Floyd's Bluff (near modern-day Sioux City, Iowa). On September 6, they encountered a trading vessel and drank their first whiskey in over a year. As each day passed, they met traders giving them news. They found that the country was deeply concerned for them, and rumors were plentiful about their status. Some thought the Corps of Discovery had been killed, while others heard they were captured by the Spanish and working as slaves in their gold and silver mines.

Nearing the End

When they were 150 miles from St. Louis, they completely ran out of provisions and trade goods. All they had left were the clothes on their backs, their rifles and ammunition, the cooking kettle, their scientific instruments, and their precious journals. On September 20, the sight of a cow on a hillside triggered spontaneous shouts of joy.

When they reached St. Charles, the village from which where they had started, the men were granted permission to fire a salute from the cannon. Their three rounds were answered with three rounds from the trading boats on the bank. The citizens rushed out to greet them, having believed they had long been lost. As celebrations began that would last for many days, Lewis immediately went on to St. Louis to rush his report to President Jefferson.

As Lewis paddled onto the Mississippi, he felt a deep sense of satisfaction at the completion of their epic voyage. He had taken a multi-cultural group of thirty unruly soldiers and guides, molding them into the Corps of Discovery. They had become a tough, hardy, resourceful crew of well-disciplined men (and a teenage woman and her baby). Covering 8,000 miles, he brought the entire party back safely, except for one man who died for causes beyond his control.

His passion for the mission never failed him. At the critical moments, he made mostly wise decisions. He found the most direct route across the continent, just as Jefferson had ordered, and gathered invaluable scientific data, adding 178 new plants to the world's knowledge. Against great odds, he returned the specimens and journals safely, including a live prairie dog. What was previously a blank part of the North American map was now filled in.

Adapting to Win

The Expedition experienced thrilling adventures, ominous mountains, terrible portages, turbulent rapids, and heartbreaking disappointments. He had conflicts with his men and conflicts with indigenous tribes. He faced every kind of physical challenge including extreme cold, mosquitoes, disease, a gunshot wound, and gas-producing roots.

They weathered mind-numbing boredom at Clatsop, and terrifying fear at the falls of the Columbia. They saw a variety of animals, trees, rivers, canyons, cliffs, and Native tribes that no one had seen before. All this was done under the cloud of apparent clinical depression.

As he pulled up to shore in St. Louis, Lewis shouted to someone on the bank, "When is the next mail leaving St. Louis?" Lewis's report read: "In obedience to your orders we have penetrated the Continent of North America to the Pacific Ocean and sufficiently explored the interior of the country to affirm with confidence that we have discovered the most practicable route which does exist across the continent."

Jefferson received the report with pride, saying: "Of courage undaunted, possessing a firmness and perseverance of purpose which nothing but impossibilities could divert from its direction, careful as a father of those committed to this charge, yet steady in the maintenance of order and discipline, I could have no hesitation in confiding the enterprise to him."

This amazing adventure had come to successful completion.

****

Why did Lewis and Clark decide to make further explorations on the way home? They could have returned the way they came, using their previous experience to ensure safe delivery of the journals and reports. They did so because of their spirit of exploration, their desire for more discovery and achievement for their Commander-In-Chief. In the same way, God has equipped you with the desire to produce a greater return on investment for His Kingdom.

Like the Corps of Discovery, if you adapt to win like they did, your journey from prison to civilian life will come to successful completion. It might not feel like it happens on a specific day or time, but there will come a time when you are confident in your cultural shift from incarceration to effective Kingdom service on the outside.

In this journey, which will take 12-18 months or more, you will face many uncertainties, but one thing is certain: The God who was with Moses, Nehemiah, Paul, and Esther is also with you! He still intervenes in the lives of His people through compelling context, detailed preparations, danger and disappointment, setbacks and suffering, decisive action, dead vision and then renewed vision, daring perseverance, patience and caution, with courage to the end.

Climbing Up

Conclusion

The Expedition required planning, adjustments, bravery, patience, and wisdom. If you finish strong and stay faithful in your re-entry journey like they did, it will be time to celebrate. Paul could say at the end of his life, "I have fought the good fight, I have finished the race, I have kept the faith" (2 Tim. 4:7). May it be so when you finish Climbing Up!

Questions for Reflection

1. Study these passages and reflect on how God's people celebrated the completion of His work: Nehemiah's wall (Neh. 8) and Crossing the Jordan (Josh. 4).

2. How do you feel when you hear that the journey of re-entry will take 12-18 months or more?

3. Review the chapter titles for Part III (Adapt to Win) and list at least one helpful idea for each chapter as you make your plans for re-entry.

Chapter 25
Growing in Wisdom

THESE FINAL CHAPTERS ARE designed to bring together the various lessons you have studied so far, giving you practical tools for your re-entry journey.

Paul said, "Be very careful, then, how you live—not as unwise but as wise, making the most of every opportunity, because the days are evil. Therefore do not be foolish, but understand what the Lord's will is" (Eph. 5:15-17).

You need wisdom because the days are evil, confusing, uncertain, and mysterious. You will face difficult decisions, conflicting information, and unclear implications because the world is constantly changing. Even as we write, we are in the middle of COVID-19 and massive civil unrest after the murder of George Floyd. No one is sure how life will be affected from either of these events.

The adversary adapts, and so must you. The devil does not sit still or remain static, so you also must adapt to win by changing your approach under opposition and fluctuating conditions.

What is Wisdom?

While the Bible is full of principles to help you make wise decisions, it is not a rulebook providing answers to every complex situation. In fact, the principles can sometimes feel like they are in opposition to each other.

For example, we are told to have faith but also to be prudent; show mercy but act justly. You can be open to change when you should stand firm. You can stand firm when you should be open to change. There is a time to be silent and a time to speak (also see Eccl. 3:1-8).

To navigate life in light of God's truth from the Bible, you need wisdom, defined as:

Wisdom is choosing what is best among equally viable truths.

How to Get Wisdom

Wisdom starts with a humble attitude toward God and a healthy skepticism about your own judgment (Prov. 9:10). He is God and you are not. Ask Him for wisdom and He will give it (Js 1:5) and seek it through disciplined effort (Prov. 2:1-6). In addition, here are a few helpful ideas in your pursuit.

Understand the Big Picture

In order to discern God's will, you need a clear understanding of His grander purposes in history. If you start from your own perspective, it is too small a reference point to give you guidance. You will become confused, overestimating your importance, and lose your way. It is better to start with what is important to God on a cosmic level, and then see how you intersect with His grand design.

Navigators never use their own location as a reference point, but use fixed points like the North Pole, the sun, or the North Star. In the same way, you should never start with your own experience to discern God's will. Instead you should use God's unchanging plan, revealed in his Word, as your fixed reference point.

The Kingdom of God was Jesus' chief concern.[36] He instructed us to "seek first His Kingdom" (Mt. 6:33) and all things would be added to us. The Kingdom involves three aspects: rescuing a people to become his own (Col. 1:13-14), destroying the work of the devil (1 Jn. 3:8), and bringing glory to God through the Son (Eph. 1:10, 22, 1 Cor. 15:24-25).

One day the kingdoms of the world will become the Kingdom of our Lord and of his Christ, and He will reign for ever and ever (Rev. 11:15.) Your life needs to be oriented around His Kingdom purposes.

Be a Living Sacrifice

When you understand the Big Picture, you recognize your role is to represent Christ in the world, being "transformed into the likeness of his Son" (Rom. 8:29). When you surrender yourself to the work of representing Christ and his Kingdom, no matter the cost, you are in a place to begin understanding his will.

Rom. 12:1-2 says: "Therefore, I urge you brothers, in view of God's mercy, to offer your bodies as living sacrifices, holy and pleasing to God–this is your spiritual act of worship. Do not conform any longer to the pattern of this world, but be transformed by the renewing of your mind. Then you will be able to test and approve what God's will is—his good, pleasing and perfect will."

Make yourself a living sacrifice, saying "Yes, Lord," even before you have heard your assignment. Do not negotiate your obedience, but surrender to His will, whatever it may be.

Grow in Intimacy with Christ

As you try your best to be a living sacrifice, and grow in your knowledge of Christ, you will learn to recognize His voice from the static of worldly voices. John White said, "Though the Bible never uses the word guidance, it does talk about a Guide. You may seek guidance, but God desires to give something better: himself."[37] As you walk with Christ and get to know Him better, your ability to discern His voice sharpens. You learn what pleases Him. Jesus said, "My sheep know my voice" (Jn. 10:27).

Jesus sent the Counselor, the Holy Spirit, to "teach us all things" and remind us of everything Jesus said (Jn. 14:26). He leads us in making God-honoring decisions, but also comforts us in our distress. We have a Guide who gives both direction and comfort. As you grow in intimate knowledge of God through trust in the Holy Spirit, you improve in your ability to discern God's will for your specific situation.

Apply Scripture

Your primary source of guidance should come from Scripture. "All Scripture is God-breathed and is useful for teaching, rebuking, correcting and training in righteousness, so that the man of God may be thoroughly equipped for every good work" (2 Tim. 3:16).

Many questions are already answered in the Bible. "How can a young man keep his way pure? By living according to your Word. I have hidden your Word in my heart, that I might not sin against you" (Ps. 119:9, 11). It is essential to be diligent in your study of the Word so you will know His mind. The Spirit speaks through the Bible, and He will never direct you in contradiction to His written Word.

Discern Your Passions and Gifts

While God can reveal His will in a direct way, as He did with people like Moses and Noah, He often reveals his will through the passions we develop for ministry. David built the temple out of his own heart for God. Hezekiah organized a large Passover celebration, motivated by his gratitude toward God. You also can develop hundreds of innovative ways to worship God and make Him known, so take your creative passions seriously.

God will use your gifts and interests to accomplish His task. God gifts all believers for works of service, to build up the body (Rom. 12:3-8, 1 Cor. 12, Eph. 4:11-13). While God is the giver of gifts and can give anyone new gifts at any time, you typically will be guided into assignments based on your past gifting. You can often recognize God's guiding hand if it involves something within your past gifting.

An especially important sign is persistent discontent with an existing situation. Remember David's words about the temple: "Here I am living in this house of cedar while the ark of God sits in a tent" (2 Sam. 7:2). Your dissatisfaction with the present state of affairs may be a good indication of something God wants to do through you.

Listen to the Body

Having placed yourself under authority of a godly church body, pay careful attention to your leaders. You need to submit to their authority since they are responsible for your well-being. "Obey your leaders and submit to their authority. They keep watch over you as men who must give an account. Obey them so that their work will be a joy, not a burden, for that would be of no advantage to you" (Heb. 13:17).

If you have a vision for ministry and your church leaders do not confirm God's leading in it, pay particular careful attention to this "red flag." God can make His will clear through the affirmation (or lack of affirmation) of godly leaders over you.

Climbing Up

You can easily deceive yourself about your own motives. You can trick yourself into thinking something is of God when it really comes from your own desires. The idea may feel selfless and you may "feel a peace" about it after time of prayer or fasting. But your feelings are not the best barometer of God's will. You can still fool yourself into doing what you want, even after sincere prayer and reflection on God's Word.

This is why you need the input of brothers and sisters who know you well and can separate out your intentions. "The heart is deceitful above all things and beyond cure" (Jer. 17:9). "No one is good, not even one" (Rom. 3:12). Seek out counsel from brothers and sisters in Christ before making a decision. "Plans fail for lack of counsel but with many advisors they succeed" (Prov. 15:22). The friends who know you can have great insight to help you discern God's will.

When you consider the counsel others, remember that you are making the final decision. You are responsible before God for your own actions. Do not blame counselors for their advice by saying, "They made me do this" or "They would not let me do that." Make the choice and live with the outcome.

Other Signs

Many people look at circumstances and say, "It must be God's will–look what is happening." Be very careful about basing God's guidance on circumstances alone. A closed door may mean you need perseverance to open it. An open door could be a tempting distraction. Circumstances might be a helpful indicator, but they ought to be the last and least of all the measures to discern God's will.

God can also speak through secular sources, or even the counsel of non-Christians. While it is good to be open to advice from any source, be skeptical by measuring it against the more reliable sources of Scripture and other believers.

Learn from Past Mistakes

Much of your experience in discerning God's will, and hearing his voice, comes through years of learning from past mistakes. When you act on something, God can reveal in hindsight that you were really acting out of your own motivations, rather than God's. But He is gentle with you, using those opportunities to help you grow. Because God can redeem your mistakes, you should be bold in trying things for Him. Do not let fear rule you.

Wisdom of the Ages

Finally, study the wisdom of other believers who have gone before you. Men and women have spent decades learning to walk with God and have written down their experiences for our benefit. The practice of wisdom is a lifetime process and worthy of much study. Two excellent resources are Henry Blackaby's book *Experiencing God*[38] and *Devotional Classics* by Richard Foster.[39]

Conclusion

Search the Scriptures for the Big Picture and specific guidance; be a living sacrifice as you grow in intimacy with Christ; listen to the Spirt who gives passions and gifts; get counsel from the saints and others; draw upon the wisdom of your past mistakes.

Trusting God to guide you, even through your mistakes, is the key to discerning His will. After carefully considering all these factors, if you do not receive clear direction, make the best decision you know to make and move ahead. "Trust in the Lord with all of your heart and lean not on your own understanding. In all your ways acknowledge Him, and He will make your path straight" (Prov. 3:5-6).

Questions for Reflection

1. Consider the nine principles of learning wisdom listed above. For each one, describe an example where you applied the principle well or ignored it and it turned out badly. (If you cannot find examples for each of the nine, ask a friend or two for examples).

2. Put the principles in order from #1-9 in terms of how much they are already a part of your thinking and decision making.

3. Think through your re-entry plan. For each of the nine principles, imagine a decision you will need to make where that principle would be helpful.

Chapter 26
PWR: An "Adapt to Win" Framework

ONCE YOU ARE COMMITTED to walking in wisdom, the following three-step framework Don developed (called PWR©) will help you revise your plans. This is an acronym for "Prepare, Work, and Review," and it is designed to help you every time you face difficulty or changes in circumstances. A disciplined use of this tool will help you take control of your situation so you do not have to feel like a victim.

You can use PWR in major decisions and big projects that go on for months or years, or it can be applied to a simple decision that needs to be made in a few minutes. The outline below goes into greater detail for use in a major project, so when you apply it to a simple situation, make sure you do not get bogged down in the details.

Pwr: PREPARE

Set the Context

"It is not good to have zeal without knowledge, nor to be hasty and miss the way" (Prov. 19:2).

1. The single most important aspect of adapt to win is to seek God. Everything starts by humbly seeking God and listening for His guidance. "God opposes the proud but gives grace to the humble" (Js. 4:6).

2. The next step is to understand the context. The context helps us interpret Bible passages; just as good decisions are made within a proper context. Seek to be like "the men of Issachar, who understood the times and knew what Israel should do" (1 Chron. 12:32).

Climbing Up

   A. Examine the history leading up to this event, then list what is happening in your situation. What led up to this decision or problem? How did you get here?

   B. List the resources you have at your disposal.

   C. List the issues that are beyond your control but affect this decision or project.

3. List 3-5 values that will guide you in making this decision. These are the non-negotiables, guiding principles, planning assumptions, or essential commitments that will guide your future decisions. For example, when the Expedition chose a location for the winter on the Pacific, they selected three criteria to guide their decision (close to game for food; near the ocean to spot a possible passing ship and supplies; a convenient place to refine salt from the ocean).

   This is a good example of how values will guide you in your decisions. Values are important because when you are overwhelmed with details, they help you stay focused on what is truly important. They help you say "no" to one thing but "yes" to another.

4. Write down the task or decision before you so it is clear. For Lewis and Clark, their task was *to find the best water route from the Mississippi River to the Pacific Ocean.* Writing this down will make clear what you are trying to do. It is common to mix several different goals or decisions together, which only causes confusion. It is best to separate them out and consider each on its own.

5. If you have a team around you, make sure you clearly communicate both the task and the values so everyone involved is on the same page. Clear direction minimizes confusion, so each person can make their contribution to the outcome.

PWR: An "Adapt to Win" Framework

Choose a Strategy

"A simple man believes anything, but a prudent man gives thought to his steps. A prudent man sees danger and takes refuge, but the simple keep going and suffer for it" (Prov. 14:15; 22:3).

1. Once you have set the context, with clear values and a defined task, the temptation will be to choose the first, most obvious strategy. Instead, dream about various options or get counsel from others until you get a variety of alternatives to consider. Suspend the tendency to jump into action. Take some reasonable time to consider the options. "Make plans by seeking advice; if you wage war, obtain guidance" (Prov. 20:18).

2. Having considered alternative strategies, the next temptation is to *try all of them*. Instead, <u>narrow</u> your options and evaluate them in terms of your available resources.

3. Finally, select the strategy from among the alternatives.

Give Assignments

". . . He gave me understanding in all the details of the plan ... be strong and courageous and do the work" (1 Chron. 28:19-20).

Finally, make a to-do list so you (and your teammates) are not left guessing about the specifics of their assignment, including a due date. Do this for yourself and for others who are helping you. Make sure you schedule a time when you will review the results of your plan, which should be done at least every three months (quarterly).

pWr: WORK

There comes a time to stop planning and start working the plan. Planning is important, but you cannot evaluate the value of a plan until you test it in real life. Your plan will probably need to be changed right away. Winning sports teams know they will have to adjust their plans at half-time.

Watch for two opposite extremes as you adapt to win. One danger is a rigid commitment to the plan despite the changing conditions. The other is a lack of discipline to follow the plan that has been put in place. Some hold on too long; others give up too easily. There is no easy answer. It takes godly wisdom to know when to stay focused and when to go in a different direction.

You have to adapt to win in the middle of the battle.

PwR: REVIEW

As you execute your re-entry plan, make sure you review your progress periodically. You should do this frequently at first (daily or weekly) and then at least quarterly until it is complete.

Working your plan is tiring and time consuming, so you may feel like the last thing you want to do is review your activity. It is easier to assume (or hope) that what you did was effective. But fruitfulness requires relentless evaluation. Since friction occurs (things seldom go according to plan), it is important to review your results so you can make corrections going forward.

The United States military has a commitment to evaluating every mission, believing the most important part of a battle is the debrief. Margaret Wheatley said, "[The Army] has this wonderful process of learning from direct experience called 'After Action Review,' in which everyone involved sits down and discusses three questions: What happened? Why do you think it happened? And what can we learn from it?"[40]

Failures are inevitable, and even valuable, when you are willing to learn from them. The most devastating defeats can be fertile ground for improvement. Jack Welch said, "Crises teach us where the system is broken and how to repair it so it won't break again...Disasters, in business and in nature, have the potential to make the organizations that survive them so much stronger in the long run."[41]

Perhaps the most important part of Review is to have a sense of humor. Because God is with you, you can relax. Even when the results are disappointing, your work has not been wasted. You cannot always see the whole picture of what God has in mind, but you can always find something to celebrate.

THE CYCLE

After REVIEW, go back to repeat the three steps of PREPARE: 1) Set the context; 2) Choose a strategy; 3) Make assignments. If you get bogged down, go back to your 3-5 values to help you. They serve as a compass when you get lost in the details so you can find your way forward.

Then WORK the plan, and then REVIEW the results. Prepare, Work, Review (PWR) is the simple structure that will help you adapt to win. You need to revise your plans because they seldom work out the way you think.

Dwight Eisenhower, leader of the Allied Forces in World War II, knew that the *process of planning* was more important than *the plan itself.* Plans can be thrown out, but the process of thinking and discussing imaginative ideas is critical. He said, "In preparing for battle, I have always found that plans are useless, but planning is indispensable."[42]

Climbing Up

Conclusion to Part III: Adapt to Win

The Lewis and Clark Expedition was full of surprises, changes of plan and adjustments, but ended in victory and celebration. In the same way, you will need to revise your re-entry plans along the way, because of friction (seldom will things go according to plan).

Climbing Up requires that you recognize culture, remember your identity in Christ, and adapt to win. You can do it under the Lord's guidance and provision, as Paul said, "And I am sure of this, that He who began a good work in you will bring it to completion at the day of Jesus Christ" (Phil. 1:6).

Questions for Reflection

1. Imagine you are Meriwether Lewis after receiving Jefferson's assignment to lead the Expedition. Using the steps listed in PWR, write an initial plan for the project.

2. Imagine you are Nehemiah after hearing about the state of Jerusalem. Using the steps in PWR, develop an initial plan to rebuild the wall. Then read on to see what he faced after starting the project and use PWR to create a new plan (see Neh. 1-6).

3. Think about your re-entry and use the steps of PWR to write an initial plan. (Appendices 1-3 have helpful ideas to get you started). Make sure you specify a time you will Review your progress!

Chapter 27
Putting It All Together

LOOK AT THE FRONT cover of the book and imagine yourself scaling the rock face to the surface. Picture yourself as that person and imagine what skills you would need to make it to the top. You have been down for a while, but now you are Climbing Up, preparing inside prison so you can start your fruitful service on the outside.

Fundamentals of Rock Climbing

Effective rock climbers suggest three fundamental skills:

1. Do not fight gravity

2. Use your legs

3. Trust your shoes.[43]

Each of these rock-climbing skills correspond to the skills you need for successful re-entry.

1. **Do not fight gravity. When you flex your biceps to hang, you fight against gravity, wasting energy. It is better to extend your arms out straight so the weight of your body hangs on your skeleton, not on your arm muscles.**

In the same way, when you use your C_p biceps to muscle your way through free-world culture, you fight against gravity that wastes your energy. It is better to recognize the new civilian culture to which you now belong and adapt to it. By doing so, you put the weight on society's "skeleton," conserving your energy rather than fighting battles you cannot win.

Of course, you do not want to give in to worldly values that lead you to sinful behavior, but whenever you can adapt to the way the culture does things, the easier it will be for you to make your re-entry transition. Remember that culture is rarely right or wrong but neutral from God's perspective. But with the help of the Christian community, you can make the transition to civilian culture!

2. <u>Use your legs.</u> **They have more muscle than your arms and are more effective at moving you up the wall.**

When you remember your identity in Christ, you tap into His strength. He has the muscle to move you up the wall. Recall the three rules of the Christian life: identity, identity, identity. Remember who you are. Remember who He is.

3. <u>Trust your climbing shoes.</u> **They help you adjust to difficult rock-climbing situations.**

As you make plans, you will face unforeseen difficulties, so you must adapt to win. The Spirit will help you revise your plans, getting a new foothold for your feet at every step.

Other Resources

To receive more instruction in these three skills, we recommend four of our other books that go into greater depth in each of these areas: *The Onesimus Workshop* (prison and civilian culture), *Think Again* (identity in Christ), *The Heroic Venture* (adapt to win), *Fight the Good Fight of Faith* (becoming a follower of Jesus), all available at Amazon. com (and linked at www.completion.global).

We also recommend two books that provide additional help for re-entry:

1. *Get Out for Good: A Practical Biblical Guide for Released Prisoners and Their Families*, by Scott Stroud, 2020, Cornerstone Books, 7335 Valle Pacifico Road, Salinas, CA 93307 (also available on Amazon.com). Contact the author at www.scottkstroud.com.

2. *Spiritual Survival Guide: For Prison and Beyond*, by Fred Nelson, 2012, Inside Out Network, 1006 Gillick Street, Park Ridge, IL 60068. (also available on Amazon.com). Contact the author at www.ionillinois.net.

Here are other helpful prison and re-entry resources:

1. Prison Fellowship (www.prisonfellowship.org), 44180 Riverside Parkway, Lansdowne, VA 20176.

2. Correctional Ministries and Chaplains Association (www.cmcainternational.org), CMCA c/o Institute for Prison Ministries, Billy Graham Center, Suite 418, 501 College Avenue, Wheaton, IL 60187.

3. Firm Foundations Ministries (www.firmfoundationsministries.org/), PO Box 8628, Wichita, KS 67208.

4. The Urban Ministry Institute (www.tumi.org), 3701 E. 13th Street, Wichita, KS 67208.

5. If you need help finding a church upon your release, look at the No Place Left network of churches (http://www.noplaceleft.net/#location).

6. Crossroads Prison Ministries (www.cpministries.org/contact), PO Box 900, Grand Rapids, MI 49509-0900.

Climbing Up

If you want to find out what it means to become a follower of Jesus, see Appendix 7, and if you are curious about what led us to write *Climbing Up*, see Appendix 8.

Above all, remember the Lord is with you in your journey! God bless you as you are Climbing Up!

About the Authors

Completion Global, Inc. is a Christian ministry dedicated to catalyzing collaborations and introducing innovations for the Great Commission. Founded in 2018, its mission is to mobilize the whole Church to its Kingdom purpose by getting every member involved, so every people group will be included. (Eph. 4:16, Mt. 24:14).

Don Allsman is the CEO of Completion Global, Inc. He served as Vice President of World Impact for 27 years, a ministry dedicated to empowering the U.S. urban poor through evangelism, discipleship, church planting, and leadership development. He led the expansion of The Urban Ministry Institute (TUMI) by forming over 250 partnerships in 12 years into 14 countries. He now serves on the advisory board of the Correctional Ministries and Chaplains Association and has authored five books used to train leaders in the inner city and in prisons. He earned an MBA and a BS in Industrial Engineering before working in aerospace and management consulting.

Cathy Allsman is the *Vice President of Prison Ministries Mobilization* for Completion Global. From 2012-2018, she served as *Incarceration Ministries Specialist* for World Impact, having expanded TUMI's ministry training program to 70 prison locations in 12 states. She has an MA in Communicative Disorders and worked for several years as a research and clinical audiologist at The House Ear Clinic, publishing articles and contributing to cutting-edge advancements in hearing technology.

Completion Global, Inc.
4261 E. University Drive, #337
Prosper, TX 75071
www.completion.global
info@completion.global

Climbing Up

Appendix 8 describes ministry training offered through The Urban Ministry Institute (TUMI). One of our goals is to see a prison TUMI site in all 50 states by the year 2025, and then to find places of service for TUMI-trained prisoners when they get out. We encourage you to talk to your chaplain or a someone you know on the outside so they can find out how to start a TUMI site in your prison. They can find out more at: www.tumi.org/satellite-services/start-a-satellite.

Appendices

Appendix 1
Testimonies of Former Prisoners

The following testimonies illustrate the complexities and challenges of re-entry, showing how tough it can be to make the transition from prison to life on the outside. As you read them, think about examples relating to the three skills of Climbing Up: recognizing cultural differences, remembering your identity in Christ, and adapt to win (revising your plans).

Think about how each person would have been helped by mastering the three skills, and how you could have handled their situations differently. Lastly, keep in mind that the testimonies are based on the state where they were released, and each state can have different situations that may not apply in your case.

Dan's Story[44]

About six months before I went home it occurred to me that I was really going home. I became very anxious. Everything started bothering me. Inmates were driving me nuts. I found new hatred for the guards. Standing in chow lines made my heart pound. And if I couldn't get on the phone when I wanted to, I about lost my mind. The funny thing was that I knew all of these attitudes were my problem. I knew nothing had changed with my surroundings; something must have changed in me. I knew I had short timer's disease.

I took some action. I prayed about it, going so far as to praying for the inmates and guards I was getting angry at. I talked about it in my recovery meetings and with fellow believers. These things helped but didn't seem to take it away. About five minutes after I woke up each day my brain would start with anxiety and resentment.

It was so surprising to me to feel so stressed about going home. I felt more stressed about leaving than I did about coming to prison.

Climbing Up

For a long time, it had been easier for me to focus on daily prison life. I really didn't want to think about the family, women, and friends that I'd left behind. That was too painful for me. To me, leaving prison was going to be the end of all my problems. I pictured a warm welcome from family, old friends, past girlfriends. I figured that someone would give me a job.

In prison, I did a lot of working out so my physical health was good. Most importantly, in prison I'd prayed, read the Bible, and was involved in a 12 Step program. I really believed that going home would be like going to Disneyland. No more crazy inmates, guards, staff. No more "celly problems." No more waiting for money in the mail or commissary. I was going to actually be free! In my deepest heart, I believed that my transition would be filled with stress-free laughter and goodwill from the world. Nothing could have been further from the truth.

Prayer definitely helped during this time and so did talking with fellow believers, people I could trust. They advised that I continue to pray, read the Bible, and find others to help, even if helping meant nothing more than a short, kind word or deed.

On the way home I got car sick. I hadn't been in a car for years and motion made me ill. As soon as I arrived at my parents' house I was filled with a sense of guilt and shame. I didn't know what exactly do next. All of the bright color of everyday life in the real-world sort of scared me. Right away I felt like I didn't fit.

Some good friends came by, friends who are sober and walking in a spiritual path. I knew they'd understand just what I was going through. They didn't. How could they? They'd never been to prison for years like I just had. They were a bit confused as to why I seemed uptight. I tried to explain but was not sure myself. I mean, "Wow, I'm actually home. So why do I feel so weird and afraid?"

I was honest with everyone. I told my friends and family that being home was like being in some alien landscape, that I didn't know what to do with my hands. After a few days I began to notice people sort of losing interest in the novelty of Dan being home. I wanted to call everyone and say, "Hey, don't lose interest, I'm home now and want to be part of life!" People just got on with their lives, and I felt alone and afraid. I literally didn't know what I should be doing every day.

I had a basic understanding that I needed to continue my sobriety through spiritual channels. To me that meant daily prayer, Bible reading, AA, and basic "golden rule" living. I did some of that, but to be honest I did more worrying about what people thought about me and where I was going to find a job. My relationship with God quickly went on the back burner.

I kept saying to myself, "Look what you have done with your life! How will you ever repair it? How will you ever get a job? And what's up with my girl? She seems to be acting weird." It was like at every turn, I felt more and more out of place. Even those old friends seemed unsure about what to say to me. I felt like the world had a secret it wouldn't let me in on. I began to unravel.

We all want to feel connected with God and people. There's nothing worse than feeling alone. After a few weeks home I felt more alone than when I was in prison. My friends in recovery were busy with family, work, and school. At church I felt little in common with these God people. I know the pastor says they don't judge, but who doesn't judge? Are there people who really don't judge? So down I went.

Climbing Up

In hindsight I missed the turn when I began to care more about what people thought about me than what I was actually doing in my life. My focus became about what I thought others were thinking about me, rather than just doing my very best to do the next right thing. My mind ran round and round, and I forgot the lessons that had been beaten into me by life in prison (and my search for God). I was back to relying on my own broken thinking.

After a serious relapse I knew I had to find a way to really stay on track. Lots of us got off the path many times. The real deal is to stay on it when the going gets tough and uncertain. I moved into a half-way house. I began to see that my troubles are about me and not about how the world treated me. I saw that I needed to put real effort into getting positive results if I wanted any. For most of my life I'd found ways of manipulating people to build the life that I wanted. I was always more interested in looking good than doing good. I saw that attitude had to stop.

Greg's story

My advice is to please stay prayerful and remain hopeful. God's got you. While nothing was as I was told, I am blessed! So amazingly, wonderfully blessed! For starters, initially I had no housing. I was homeless but got into a sober-living bed through B.I. (Behavioral Interventions), a division of GEO Corp. I also signed up with Veterans Community Services for housing assistance, but B.I. got me housed first. The Lord has shown me much favor, including showing me the spot where I slept when I was homeless.

I got EBT asap, which typically is $194 every month. Once I got the EBT card and an I.D. card I was able to get an "Obama phone," with unlimited talk and text plus 500 MB data. As a homeless EBT recipient I was able to go to several fast food restaurants to eat hot meals. I only go to the office for monthly UA's. Employment was sporadic, but I got hired here at the Plaza Hotel one year ago, and I am full-time, working front desk two days per week and three days maintenance. God is good, all the time!

Additionally, I see God bringing healing in my family relationships, including my wife. I know He is working behind the scenes, and occasionally gave me glimpses to bolster my faith.

Now as to the where I am with regard to the local Body of Christ. God has me on a mission. He has opened the doors for me to encourage others and lay the foundation for continued support and future ministry. God connected me to a TUMI brother in ministry and I have opportunities to share at those services. I wrapped up my ninth module in TUMI, and I hope to complete the program. I have received manifold blessings. I am blessed by the best! Woo-Hoo!

All in all, I've had some challenges, and with that some periods of depression and extreme sadness. Yet, at the end of the day, God is faithful. He always comes through, if not on my schedule. His grace is my provision. Without it I would not be doing as well as I am.

Stay prayerful, stay hopeful, and stay connected to the Body. For "In Him we live and move and have our being' as even some of your own poets have said, 'For we are indeed his offspring'" (Acts 17:28). "For this reason I also suffer these things; nevertheless I am not ashamed, for I know whom I have believed and am persuaded that He is able to keep what I have committed to Him until that Day" (2 Tim. 1:11-13, NKJV).

Climbing Up

Martin's story

I am writing to tell you a little about my re-integration into society after 22 years California State Prison. I was scheduled to go to a home upon release, but a week before my parole I was told I would be going to another place. To tell the truth I was very disappointed at this change which was out of my control.

Next, I was told that I would not be picked up by the agency and would have to take the train and bus (it was actually two trains and two buses). Furthermore, when I asked my counselor to call and ask how I would make it to the program from the train station, I was told to just get a taxi or something. I was now devastated and disappointed.

This background information is written to explain what I've found to be most important about coming back to society after being in prison for so long and it's building relationships and networking. I was blessed when I arrived at the train station (8 pm on Sunday night) to have two ex-lifers, who I served with in ministry within prison, pick me up. These men helped me to navigate all of the many different roads I would have to travel in order to get "established" as a returning citizen.

Some things that are necessary and important: 1) You are going to need ID. If you don't have your birth certificate (have your family) order it. If you had a Driver License that's less than 25 years old you may still be in the system. 2) You're going to need a Social Security Card (you need a California ID or DL for this). 3) Patience!

All the programs are different. Whether they grant day passes, let you use your phones, take you to appointments, are of little consequence. Eventually, you will be granted access and opportunities to move around, explore, and it will be up to you to make good and wise decisions.

Seek out a group of knowledgeable people to help you! Seek out the lifers groups, ministries, and parole resources set in place to help you. Be open and honest with you parole agent! Call him often and ask a lot of questions! Be persistent and don't take "no" for an answer! Use the library and career center to help you. Learn to use computers and the internet.

Above all, get hooked up with God's people. Find a good church home. I hope this was helpful. Be thankful to God for your freedom. Do God's Will and let Him guide you through His Holy Spirit day by day.

Kevin's Story

This is from an ex-lifer that just did twenty-seven years in California. I have been out six months. I do not have all the answers, so let me share with you what I do know.

I will tell you everything has changed. I will tell you that the worst day out here, is still better than the best day in there. Just as you worked for your parole date, you also have to work to be on parole. The best advice I can give to you is to keep a tally of all the money you spend because it doesn't last long.

If you were in prison for less than twenty-five years, you just pay a renewal fee for your driver license it is still active. If you were incarcerated for over twenty-five years you are no longer in the system. The first thing you have to do then is to acquire a birth certificate at the county hall of records.

Climbing Up

Then second thing you will need is a Social Security card. A DD-214 will work if you are a veteran. In acquiring your California I.D. as a birth certificate, you will also have to take the CDL written exam and the driver's test with a vehicle. Once you have done this you should receive your CDL + Social Security Card within a few weeks. When you are released you will also qualify for Medical. Always remember to try to have a positive attitude.

We are more concerned about what people think of us or about us than they actually do. Remember the Word of the Lord. It will always help you through if you are sincere about your new walk in life. There is an abundance of people who want to help so just ask. Be humble, honest, gracious, and patient.

One day a couple weeks after you get out, it will hit you that your truly free. I will tell you if you have a brother or a sister in the Church to call, then do it. They will give words of encouragement, support, and comfort.

The world out here is fleshly everywhere you turn. Everywhere you go there are sex and drugs. I can tell you if you don't stay grounded in faith, the desires of the worldly man will eat you.

I will say that surrounding yourself with like-minded brothers and sisters will help you stay grounded. Life is fast and expensive out here, but it is doable. Find a solid base. Remember the Word of the Lord. It's not easy because there is no down time out here; you must set time for yourself.

Now that you have completed the first part of the race by getting yourself paroled the race in not over it has just begun.

Appendix 2
Tips for Re-entry

The Cell Church
"The word of God is not imprisoned."
                    – 2 Timothy 2:9

Mark Walker
Success in Parole

I completed 10 years of parole in 2018, and have been doing well by God's grace, ever since. When asked how I've been successful since being paroled, I don't really know what to say. I'm amazed at how far the Lord has brought me, and I know I still have a long way to go. A lot of people other than me have contributed to my success. However, there are a few things I found helpful that I can share with you. You may find that concentrating on as many of these areas as you can, will help you to lay a strong foundation for your return to the community.

1. Advance Preparation

You will need to prepare more than just a parole plan in order to give yourself the best opportunity for success. Begin thinking as early as possible about opportunities you can pursue now which will help you prepare for life on the streets. In order to do this, you will need to develop a vision for your future and set some goals that will help you move toward that vision.

For example, I knew I wanted to go back to college when I got out. In order to do that, I would need to be able to find a stable, decent paying job as soon as possible where I could work while I went to school. So, I got some feedback from other people about what I was good at. An attorney who had represented me suggested I would make a good paralegal, so I found a school where I could get a paralegal certificate through correspondence. I earned the certificate, and that same attorney hired me when I was paroled. Having a stable job enabled me to cover my living and parole expenses, and to go back to college. I graduated from Moody Bible Institute in about four years, and then was able to go on to seminary and am working on a doctorate degree. So, the preparation I did on the inside enabled me to be successful in school when I got out.

It is also very important to work at maintaining as many relationships as possible while you are down. I made it a point to stay in touch with my family as much as I could, and I wrote regularly to a pastor at a church in Denver. Not only did this keep me engaged with what was going on outside, but I was also prepared with a network of supportive relationships with people who were able and willing to help me when I was released.

2. Detailed Planning

I found it extremely helpful to carefully think through everything about my upcoming parole that I could. I just sat on my rack and brainstormed every possible situation I might face or need I might have when I got out. Then I made lists of everything I needed to do in the following areas:

   A. Parole – I listed tasks I would need to accomplish right away and questions I wanted to ask my parole officer during our first meeting

   B. Basic documents – I thought of all the personal documents I would need to get, especially a drivers' license and a social security card

C. Setting up my life – I thought through how I would go about collecting and transporting whatever personal belongings others had kept for me

D. Financial – I thought through what I would need to do to set up bank accounts, get a debit card and personal checks

E. Priorities – I thought through the goals I had made for my vision of the future (like going back to school), and then I listed in order the steps I would need to take toward accomplishing those goals.

Once I had my lists, I tried to prioritize everything in order of importance, so the first things on my list would be the ones I would need to do right away when I got out. I kept these lists with me and referred to them often during the first few months of my parole.

3. Managing Finances

Parole can be demanding, not only of your time but your money as well, depending on what your conditions are. It is therefore very important to avoid all unnecessary financial stress. As soon as I got a job and knew what my income and expenses would be, I immediately worked to create a detailed and prioritized budget. If you've never made a budget, I strongly recommend you learn how; there are probably books in the facility library that will teach you. I also made it a point to keep track of everything I spent, and to carefully balance my checkbook and reconcile my bank accounts regularly. The point is – watch your money closely, so you can be sure you will have what you need to pay for the most important things in your life – housing, parole expenses, transportation, etc.

It is also important to think about how you will build your credit. If you have been down for a while you may have no credit at all – not bad, not good. This is actually a great place to start if you do it right. I quickly got a low-limit credit card. It had a high interest rate, but I only used it to buy gas and then paid it off every month with the money I had in my budget for gas. Just by doing that I was able to build a really good credit rating pretty quickly, without borrowing a lot of money or paying any interest. That was a huge help a few years ago, when I was finally ready to buy a house. I had no problem getting a loan, because my credit was great.

4. Family Support

It is certainly possible to be successful on parole without family support, but if you do have committed family supporting you it is an incredible gift. Their support while you are on the inside can give continuity to your transition because the relationships remain relatively stable. Also, their support on the outside can make your obstacles much smaller in the areas of transportation, housing, and finances. Of course, relying on your family's help in any of these areas for too long can quickly put a strain on your relationships. However, if your family can help you to alleviate these kinds of stresses in the first few months after you are released, it can greatly increase your potential for success. If you have no family to support you, I recommend doing what you can to invest in relationships with friends, ministers, and organizations on the streets who can help to fill some of that role.

5. Relationship with Your Parole Officer

There are few things more important to your success on parole than building a foundation of trust with your PO. This will be harder with some officers than with others, but you can't control what officer you are assigned or what their attitude is – you can only control how you choose to interact with them. Honesty is a priority, even if you screw up. Don't be afraid to discuss your feelings and struggles with your officer, depending on how your relationship is with them.

Remember that building trust takes time, and your PO will challenge you – especially at first – to see if you will follow their rules and whether or not you can take no for an answer, even when it doesn't make sense. Be patient, and don't demand things you think you "deserve" or get angry with them for their treatment of you. Over time, if you are cooperative and honest and you work hard to be successful, the relationship will improve. A good relationship with your PO can make your time on parole a totally different experience, so put your best effort into it.

6. Employer Support

It will be a great help if you are able to find an employer who will show you understanding and flexibility on the job. In order to have understanding, you must be up front with your potential employers about your background and your parole conditions. If you have to drop UAs you might have to leave work early or come in late. You might have to take time off for appointments with your PO, or for any treatment you are required to do. Make sure your prospective employer knows what he or she is getting into before they hire you. As long as they understand what you will need, they can tell you whether or not they can give you the flexibility to be able to take time off or adjust your schedule when needed. Do not expect parole to work around your job; try to find a job that will work around your parole. It is better to get turned down for a job up front because an employer can't be flexible, than it is to get fired later because your parole requirements are interfering with your job in ways the employer did not expect.

Climbing Up

7. Building Friendships

One of the most important things you can do when you are released is to invest in new relationships, and work to surround yourself with healthy community. This should include positive people at your job, in your faith community, and successful participants in treatment programs you may be required to attend. To be able to do this it is important to be transparent – you have to let people know the real you. You should think about sharing as much as possible with people about where you came from and what you have been through. This is particularly vital for your relationships with parole, employers, and treatment, but it is important for healthy friendships as well. A word of caution – you may find it difficult to re-establish healthy social boundaries in your relationships.

8. Pursuing Goals

The encouragement of setting and achieving goals will help keep you going when things become discouraging (and they will). Set simple short-term goals that you will be able to achieve quickly; this will help you build confidence about your ability to succeed. Set long term goals in areas you find personally important and inspiring. Looking ahead to these goals will help keep you motivated through difficulties. If you don't have much experience setting goals find someone who can help you get started; it will be a great life skill for you to have in the future.

Part of this process is celebrating your achievements, acknowledging your successes, and rewarding yourself for them. If you are like me, this could be a difficult one for you; I never felt like I had accomplished anything significant, and I didn't really know how to cope with success. I was more comfortable with failure. So, get some help with this - enlist your family and friends to point out your accomplishments and help you celebrate them.

9. Hope

Never underestimate the power of the vision of a bright future. Hope is an expectation of something coming in the future that gives us energy and motivation for today. The system we find ourselves in is not conducive to hope. It probably will not offer you much in the way of hope, so it will be important for you to find your own hope. That means working intentionally to develop a positive vision for your future. This should go beyond just setting individual goals to a big-picture idea of what you want your life to be.

10. Purpose

Seeking purpose involves building value into your life through commitment to a higher calling. You will be far more likely to succeed on parole if you are working for something bigger than yourself. Your higher calling might include a healthy fight to make things better for yourself, your friends, and your family. After I was released, I spent some time working with nonprofits which are trying to improve the prison and criminal justice systems, or to provide services for parolees. It can involve serving at your church; I was able to get involved with the worship music ministry at my home church, which gives me an arena in which I can serve others and help the church pursue its ministry vision. It can involve preparation for your vision of the future. I went back to school when I got out, and I have been able to stay committed over the years in part because I am preparing to do the best work I can for those I serve in prison ministry. You can find a sense of greater purpose in many ways. The important thing is that you commit to something bigger than yourself, which is important to you and in which you can invest your time and energy.

11. Faith

I trust that this point has been running throughout all my other points, since it is really foundational to my own experience. Strong faith can enable you to calmly cope with a system that is bigger and more powerful than you. I know a lot of my suggestions to this point might seem weak and ineffectual in the face of the massive obstacles confronting you when you are released. And of course, they are – there is a lot more to success than a few practical tips and tricks. In spite of all my planning and work, in spite of all the positive things that have happened which helped me, I would have given up a long time ago if I didn't believe there was Someone who loved me and was in control of everything that was happening to me. It's really to Him that I owe everything. If you've read all of this and are still thinking you can't do it, I encourage you to place your future in the hands of God. He can overcome any obstacle you face, and when you belong to Him, He promises to never leave you on your own, no matter what.

I pray that these thoughts have been helpful to you! Succeeding on parole will be challenging but be encouraged that you can accomplish it with supportive relationships in multiple contexts, careful thought and planning, and hope for the future arising from your goals, transcendent purpose, and faith.

****

Stages of Re-Entry
Quentin Valdois

In my experience, you start a period of time where everything seems ideal. Your loved ones are happy to have you out and everything seems new and beautiful. Eventually the beauty starts to fade. You feel a keen sense of separation between you and the culture around you. This is heightened, because you don't anticipate a cultural shift. After all, you think you're entering your native culture and have left your "prison identity" at the gate when you left prison.

You experience a high level of anxiety when placed in situations that were dangerous in prison (being in large groups of people). You may be hesitant to leave the house and be out in public at all. You easily misinterpret the actions of others. Others can't understand why it's hard for you to make decisions or why you act the way you do.

You may feel like people can tell by looking at you that you were in prison and have a sense of paranoia when you're around people you don't know. Some people start surrounding themselves with people involved in illegal activity because the culture is similar to what they experienced in prison and they feel more comfortable in that culture.

This can last for a year or more but will dissipate as you assimilate back into the dominant culture. My advice to guys getting out is not to overestimate their ability to jump back into the outside culture. I encourage them to acknowledge what they are experiencing and see it as normal. I also encourage them to press beyond what they think they can endure. Eventually things will get easier.

An example of how this works: I may take a guy to a department store to help him get some things he needs. As we walk into the store, I ask him how he's feeling and assure him that his anxiety is normal. I tell him that we can leave at any time even if we aren't finished shopping. I can always come back and get the things he needs. I encourage him, though, to stay just a little longer than he thinks he can before we leave. I encourage him to practice this every day as he goes about his everyday life. I also let him know that things get easier over time so to be patient with himself and to find the humor in how "weird" he is feeling.

The single thing that helped me when I got out of prison was the Gospel. When I struggled with internal dialog from my prison identity, I reminded myself of the work of Christ and the Truth of my identity in Him. The Great Exchange was vital to my ability to tell myself the truth and battle my internal dialog that tell me lies. Knowing Christ took my sin and gave me His perfection at salvation was key. The "already, not yet" truth of who I am and who I will eventually be revealed to be, helped me through time of doubt and discouragement. I must have turned to the Gospel hundreds of times a day. It's become a natural part of my thinking even today.

****

You can reach Mark Walker and Quentin Valdois at: *The Cell Church,* P.O. Box 351913, Westminster, CO 80035
Email: mark@thecellchurch.org, q@thecellchurch.org
Website: https://www.thecellchurch.org

Appendix 3
Forming a Plan Before Release

The following questions will help you form a plan upon your release. But remember, whatever plan you make, you will have to revise your plans!

1. Where will you attend church, or which churches will you visit upon release? How do you plan to get connected with a small group or mentor?

2. Where will you live? If you assume that friends or family are housing you, have you clearly communicated that expectation?

3. Who will pick you up at the gate?

4. What will your schedule be for the first three hours after you are released? What is your schedule for the first three days?

5. What parenting responsibilities will you have? What expectations do others have for you regarding parenting?

6. What household responsibilities will you have (chores, paying bills, transportation)? What do others expect from you in these areas?

7. What plans do you have for employment or education? If there is not a job or schooling waiting, what are your job-search plans?

8. What family or friends do you want to visit when you get out and how many hours per week are planned for these visits? How will you avoid spending too much time getting re-connected when you need to spend time on other tasks?

9. Do you have any broken relationships that need restoration, and if so, what is your plan to seek restoration?

10. What physical needs do you have such as a driver's license, birth certificate, or social security card? What can be secured before release versus what needs to be pursued after release?

11. What expectations do you have for finances, and what do others expect of you financially? Do you have a checking account?

12. What friends or family should you avoid so you can associate with only positive influences?

13. If you have substance abuse in your past, how will you be proactive to keep dealing with that, avoiding the naive notion that you are immune from temptation?

14. If you have children, how have they changed since your incarceration? What are they thinking about your release? What do you need to do in response?

15. What elements of prison culture do you see in yourself so that you can be open to correction as you shift to civilian culture?

16. What do you need to purchase, e.g. clothes, toiletries?

17. What needs to be done about filing taxes?

18. What needs to be done about child support obligations or parole requirements?

19. How will you safeguard yourself against wasting time on new technologies such as video games, online shopping, gambling, or pornography?

Appendix 4
Bible Verses About Your Identity in Christ

The following are affirmations of your identity in Christ from Victory over the Darkness[45], by Neil Anderson which you should study and review periodically to remember who you are:

1. I am Christ's friend (Jn. 15:15).

2. I am chosen and appointed by Christ to bear His fruit (Jn. 15:16).

3. I am a slave of righteousness (Rom. 6:18).

4. I am enslaved to God (Rom. 6:22).

5. I am a son of God; God is spiritually my Father (Rom. 8:14-15; Gal. 3:26; 4:6).

6. I am a joint heir with Christ, sharing His inheritance with Him (Rom. 8:17).

7. I am a temple, a dwelling place of God. His Spirit and His life dwell in me (1 Cor. 3:16; 6:19).

8. I am united to the Lord and am one in spirit with Him (1 Cor. 6:17).

9. I am a member of Christ's Body (1 Cor. 12:27; Eph. 5:30).

10. I am a new creation (2 Cor. 5:17).

11. I am reconciled to God and am a minister of reconciliation (2 Cor. 5:18-19).

12. I am a son of God and one in Christ (Gal. 3:26-28).

13. I am an heir of God since I am a son of God (Gal. 4:7).

14. I am a saint (1 Cor. 1:2; Eph. 1:1; Phil. 1:1; Col. 1:2).

15. I am God's workmanship, His handiwork, born anew in Christ to do His work (Eph. 2:10).

16. I am a fellow citizen with the rest of God's family (Eph. 2:19).

Climbing Up

17. I am a prisoner of Christ (Eph. 3:1; 4:1).

18. I am righteous and holy (Eph. 4:24).

19. I am a citizen of heaven, seated in heaven right now (Eph. 2:6; Phil. 3:20).

20. I am hidden with Christ in God (Col. 3:3).

21. I am an expression of the life of Christ because He is my life (Col. 3:4).

22. I am chosen of God, holy and dearly loved (Col. 3:12; 1 Thess. 1:4).

23. I am a son of light and not of darkness (1 Thess. 5:5).

24. I am a holy partaker of a heavenly calling (Heb. 3:1).

25. I am a partaker of Christ; I share in His life (Heb. 3:14).

26. I am one of God's living stones, being built up in Christ as a spiritual house (1 Pet. 2:5).

27. I am a member of a chosen race, a royal priesthood, a holy nation, a people for God's own possession (1 Pet. 2:9-10).

28. I am an alien and stranger in this world where I temporarily live (1 Pet. 2:11).

29. I am an enemy of the devil (1 Pet. 5:8).

30. I am a child of God and I will resemble Christ when He returns (1 Jn. 3:1,2).

31. I am born of God so the evil one, the devil, cannot touch me (1 Jn. 5:18).

32. I am not the great "I am" (Ex. 3:14; Jn. 8:24,25,58), but by the grace of God, "I am what I am" (1 Cor. 15:10).

Appendix 5
Thoughts on Spiritual Disciplines

The spiritual disciplines are a means of transformation that God wants to bring about in you (Rom. 12:1-2). They are <u>not</u> a way to earn favor with God or to merit salvation. As an ambassador of Christ, you have already earned His favor because of Christ's work, but He desires to produce a ROI through you for His Kingdom.

Dallas Willard defined the spiritual disciplines this way: "A discipline is any activity within our power that we engage in to enable us to do what we cannot do by direct effort."[46] In other words, we do the disciplines, but God does the transformation.

Like a professional athlete who has already made the team and simply wants to become a better player, you engage the spiritual disciplines to become more effective in your representation of Christ. For example, if you start playing basketball, you have certain shooting habits in your legs, arms, wrists, and fingers. You may have good shooting habits in your legs and fingers, but bad habits in your arms and wrist.

How do you improve your game? Will it be by reading a book or watching a video? No, you improve the same way NBA players improve. They find coaches who provide drills for them to do, and then they practice the drills over and over. They get rid of old bad habits and replace them with good habits through repeated practice and discipline. Steph Curry was not born dribbling and shooting the way he does, but he got that way through disciplined practice.[47]

The Holy Spirit is your coach, and if you ask Him to teach you, He will transform your habits over time to be more and more like Jesus.

Climbing Up

<u>Various Lists</u>

There is no single, authorized "list" of spiritual disciplines. Different people describe them in different ways. For example, Moreland organizes disciplines in two categories:

1. Disciplines of Abstinence: solitude, silence, fasting, frugality, chastity, secrecy, sacrifice

2. Disciplines of Engagement: study, worship, celebration, service, prayer, fellowship, confession, submission.[48]

Don Davis lists them in three categories:

1. Cultivating our Communion: The Inward Disciplines (Word, prayer, fasting, study)

2. Cultivating our Character: The Outward Disciplines (simplicity, solitude, submission, service)

3. Cultivating our Community: The Corporate Disciplines (confession, worship, guidance, celebration).[49]

<u>Sabbath</u>

One final thought on this topic relates to keeping the Sabbath. Jesus said "The Sabbath was made for man, not man for the Sabbath (Mk. 2:27), which means it is a gift from God for His creation, not a law to earn His favor. It can also be understood as a discipline, an activity that is within your power to do, which God uses to produce fruit in you.

Taking a day off from working each week has proven to be a huge blessing to us over the years, even though it takes discipline to cease from normal work. It is a temptation to think we are indispensable, and if we take a day off each week, our world would not be able to go on without our direct involvement.

We encourage you to practice the discipline of Sabbath by resting from normal work activities, and perhaps other habits that distract you from worship and rest, like social media.

Appendix 6
Practical Steps When You Feel Overwhelmed

Sometimes you can feel overwhelmed by so much information and it becomes difficult to know where to start. Everyone feels this way at times. This list might help you know what to do when you are discouraged.

1. Ask God, what should I do next? Do not try to solve everything at once. Just take the next step. Once you know the next step, do the next thing well.

2. Go back to your 3-5 values from PWR. They serve as a compass when you get lost in the details so you can find your way and move forward.

3. Pay attention to the basics. Timothy Jennings said, "Live in harmony with the physical design protocols for life, such as regular sleep, drink plenty of water, exercise mind and body regularly, avoid toxins, and eat a balanced diet. When mistakes are made, resolve guilt as soon as possible, forgive those who mistreat you, and don't hold to anger or grudges as such emotions activate the body's inflammatory cascade. Resolve fear, as unremedied fear truly destroys. It is love that heals and restores, but genuine love is only experienced when lies about God are removed."[50]

4. Shorten the response time between falling and getting up. We all fall and make mistakes, but the difference is how quickly we get up from falling. Does it take a minute, a day, a week, or a year for you to respond to God's leading and get back up on your feet?

5. To find peace and liberty, follow the advice of Thomas á Kempis:[51]

   A. Strive to give up your own rights and desires to serve others.

   B. Choose always to have less than more.

Climbing Up

C. Seek lower places in life, putting to death the need to be recognized and important.

D. Always and in everything desire that the will of God completely fulfilled in you.

Appendix 7
How to Become a Follower of Jesus

**To become a follower of Jesus is to join God in His story
of creation, incarnation, and re-creation.**

CREATION

<u>God Created</u>: **Beauty, purpose and evidence of His design are
all around us**. The Bible tells us that God originally planned a world
that worked perfectly, where everything and everyone fit together in
harmony. God made each of us with a purpose, to worship and walk
with Him. "God saw all that He had made, and it was very good"
(Genesis 1:31).

<u>We Rebelled</u>: **The first humans refused God's reign over them.**
We selfishly insisted on doing things our own way. The Bible calls this
sin. We all sin and distort God's original design. The consequence of
sin is separation from God in this life, and for all eternity. "All have
sinned and fall short of the glory of God" (Romans 3:23).

<u>We Searched</u>: **Life was not working on our own.** When we realize
life is not working, we begin to look for a way out. We tend to go in
many directions trying different things to figure it out on our own.
"They exchanged the truth of God for a lie, and worshipped and
served something created instead of the Creator" (Romans 1:25).

INCARNATION AND RE-CREATION

<u>God Initiated</u>: **Because of His love, God had a plan to win all
creation back from rebellion.** Through a chosen people (Jews),
God revealed His plan to win back what was lost in our rebellion.
He sent His Son Jesus, God in human flesh (incarnation), to live
a perfect life according to God's design. Jesus came to rescue all

creation (re-creation), doing what we could not do for ourselves. He paid the penalty for sin by His sacrificial death, restoring our relationship with God. Jesus was then raised from the dead, proving His authority to give eternal life. "For God loved the world in this way: He gave His One and Only Son" (John 3:16).

We Respond: We agree with His truth and turn away from our former life. By admitting our sinful brokenness, we stop trusting ourselves and ask God to forgive us. We turn from sin (repent) and trust only in Jesus (believe), receiving new life, a new way of living, and a new community of fellow followers of Jesus. "For you are saved by grace through faith, and this is not from yourself; it is God's gift, not from works, so that no one can boast" (Ephesians 2:8-9).

God Transforms: God changes us from the inside to be more like Jesus. As we get to know God better through the Bible and His people (the Church), He empowers us to follow His design for life, assures us of His presence, and gives us hope for eternity to come. "For it is God who is working in you, enabling you both to desire and to work out His good purpose" (Philippians 2:13).

We Represent: We are the continuation of Jesus' work on the earth. Those who follow Jesus are assigned to continue Jesus' good works as His ambassadors in the world. We love and serve others, and invite them to join His story of creation, incarnation, and re-creation. "Therefore, we are ambassadors for Christ, God making his appeal through us. We implore you on behalf of Christ, be reconciled to God" (2 Corinthians 5:20).

You Decide: If you want to join His Story through Christ, all you need to do is ask. "For everyone who calls on the name of the Lord will be saved" (Romans 10:13). You can talk to Him using

How to Become a Follower of Jesus

words like these: "My life is broken and I recognize it is because of my sin. I need you. I believe Jesus came to live, die, and rise from the dead to rescue me from my sin and make me His ambassador. Forgive me. I turn from my selfish ways and put my trust in you. I know that Jesus is God, and I will follow Him."

If you have responded to God's invitation to follow Jesus, the next step is to get to know Him better by studying the Bible so you can obey His teachings, join in regular relationship with His followers, and share what you discover with others.

Appendix 8
The Origins of *Climbing Up*

In 1990, World Impact started planting indigenously-led churches in the inner cities of America. This led to the establishment of The Urban Ministry Institute (TUMI) in 1995, offering culturally-relevant and reproducible ministry training for leaders among the urban poor who desired to be more effective as pastors, elders, deacons, and small-group leaders.

In 2005, Dr. Don Davis, the founder of TUMI, released The Capstone Curriculum, a 16-module, four-year ministry training program that could be offered in a local context, anywhere in the world. It is delivered through his teaching on DVD, led by a local facilitator. By 2006, there were 11 ministries providing Capstone training in urban communities, and one that began as an experiment in Ellsworth Prison in Kansas.

In 2007 Prison Fellowship formed a partnership with World Impact to start TUMI sites in seven California prisons. The first graduating class of this four-year program was so impressive that Wayne Hughes offered to expand Capstone in prisons throughout California and Cathy was asked to take on the role of overseeing TUMI's expansion in prisons as *Incarceration Ministries Specialist*.

Capstone proved to be effective in transforming prisoners for Christ, healing broken families, and reducing violence within the prisons. It exploded to 70 prisons in 12 states by 2018. During this time, we traveled from Alaska to Michigan, visiting dozens of prisons where Capstone was being used to train inmates. We experienced the excitement of several graduations, seeing transformation right before our eyes.

Climbing Up

As some of the TUMI students started being released from prison, we were eager to get them plugged into local churches where they could bring Christ-centered healing to the communities they once had destroyed. But we quickly learned that it was not so easy for prisoners to make that transition from prison to local churches.

They were not always welcomed by churches, and many former prisoners became discouraged in their faith when they could not find a church home. Others found it difficult to be accepted even though they were trained as ministry leaders in prison. Many felt so frustrated that they stopped looking for a church home. We were losing the fruit of TUMI's ministry.

This led us to look more deeply into the process of transition from prison to church life on the outside. We talked to dozens of former prisoners, their families, and people in re-entry ministry, learning all we could about what constituted successful transition from prison to civilian life.

From our findings, we published a two-hour video called the *Onesimus Workshop* in 2018, with the stated purpose: "To orient churches to the process of welcoming former prisoners into the life of their church for building up the Body of Christ, so that churches could be strengthened by incorporating the formerly incarcerated as assets using their gifts as redeemed ambassadors of Christ."

The central principle that we discovered in our anecdotal research was that most men and women return to prison because they are unable to make the shift from prison culture to civilian culture. In other words, it is a cultural issue, not a character issue.

The Origins of Climbing Up

This runs counter to the conventional wisdom about successful re-entry, which suggests that what former prisoners need are physical things like a job and housing. We maintain that such things are certainly important, but what people need most are friends; a community that will help them make the transition from one culture to another.

The name "Onesimus" comes from the book of Philemon, where Paul wrote a letter about Onesimus, Philemon's runaway slave. Paul had found Onesimus to be an asset in ministry. He wrote that "formerly he was useless to you, but now he has become useful to you and to me (v.11)."

Like the prisoners of today, Onesimus was not highly valued by worldly standards, but Paul found him useful. The process of transformation took a team: Paul, Onesimus, and Philemon, just as it takes a team today: the former prisoner, the local church, and disciplers on the inside.

One of our colleagues, Quentin Valdois from *The Cell Church*, shared his experience about the *Onesimus Workshop*. Quentin's father had served in prison ministry and already had a good understanding prison culture. But to get a better understanding of the cultural differences, Quentin asked his dad to watch the Onesimus Workshop videos with him.

Even though Quentin had been out for quite some time, and they both had already experienced the process of cultural transition, each of them were surprised at how much they learned about culture. Quentin said that the *Onesimus Workshop* gave words to many of the conflicts and frustrations they had experienced together during the years after his return home.

Climbing Up

In 2019, we started sharing the *Onesimus Workshop* with chaplains and our incarcerated friends. After their review, some prisoners expressed surprise that they had even been enculturated in prison and asked us if we would write a version especially for them. They told us of their desire to learn about prison and civilian culture so they could do the work to get ready for their release.

Starting with research from the *Onesimus Workshop*, we sought additional input from former prisoners about key factors for their successful re-entry. As a result of their input, we boiled it down to three fundamental skills: 1) recognize the cultural differences between prison and the outside world; 2) remember your identity in Christ; 3) revise your plans when things go wrong. This led to the publication of *Climbing Up* in 2020.

The culture skill is adapted from the *Onesimus Workshop*, the identity skill is adapted from *Think Again*, a book Don wrote in 2018, and the "revise your plans" skill is adapted from *The Heroic Venture*, a book Don wrote in 2006. To receive the full benefit in developing these skills, we recommend that you read *Think Again* and *The Heroic Venture*, both of which are available at Amazon.com.

Appendix 9
An Example Exercise to Remember Your Identity

Example #1

Pray Subordinately: Yes Lord, forge me into your identity today.

Gather Subjectively: I'm angry at the way my son is being treated at his work. I'm happy that I'm making progress on my ministry projects and it looks like I'll catch up before we travel again. I'm tired but hopeful about our finances. I feel abandoned by my friends.

Focus Objectively: I can change, I can choose happiness. I don't have to be affected by what others do or say. Praise God for all His blessings. He rolled back the oppression of Egypt and He can do the same for me.

Write Playfully: How can I get to what I know is truth? I want to be vindicated and proved right. But my vindication doesn't have to come from people, I can be vindicated by my baptism into Christ. In Him I am truly free.

Re-wire Decisively: I'm fully vindicated.

Execute Repetitively (seven repetitions): Quiet time, 10 am, noon, 3 pm, 5 pm, bedtime, wake up.

Example #2

Pray Subordinately: Let me seek your Kingdom first today. Make me like you Jesus. Forgive me for being self-centered.

Climbing Up

Gather Subjectively: Tired and angry. Lonely. I'm happy I got my taxes filed and paid. I'm running so fast to get things done, I wish I could stop going so fast.

Focus Objectively: The Kingdom is bigger than just our ministry and family. Jesus is Lord and will deal with others who need correcting. It's not my job to fix them.

Write Playfully: What is blocking me from enjoying this day? I can be transformed one degree at a time. Today can be a new step of glory and freedom. I can follow the example of Jesus who stepped into a pace of suffering leading up to the cross. In this season of Lent, I can take on a pace that is in stride with Jesus' walk to the cross.

Re-wire Decisively: Stride into Lenten Pace

Execute Repetitively (seven repetitions): Wake up, workout, go to work, lunch, yard time, dinner, bedtime

Appendix 10
Abbreviations of the Books of the Bible

Genesis	Gen.	Isaiah	Is.
Exodus	Ex.	Jeremiah	Jer.
Leviticus	Lev.	Lamentations	Lam.
Numbers	Num.	Ezekiel	Ezek.
Deuteronomy	Dt.	Daniel	Dan.
Joshua	Josh.	Hosea	Hos.
Judges	Judg.	Joel	Joel
Ruth	Ruth	Amos	Amos
1 Samuel	1 Sam.	Obadiah	Obad.
2 Samuel	2 Sam.	Jonah	Jonah
1 Kings	1 Kings	Micah	Mic.
2 Kings	2 Kings	Nahum	Nah.
1 Chronicles	1 Chron.	Habakkuk	Hab.
2 Chronicles	2 Chron.	Zephaniah	Zeph.
Ezra	Ezra	Haggai	Hag.
Nehemiah	Neh.	Zechariah	Zech.
Esther	Esther	Malachi	Mal.
Job	Job	Matthew	Mt.
Psalms	Ps.	Mark	Mk.
Proverbs	Prov.	Luke	Lk.
Ecclesiastes	Eccl.	John	Jn.
Song of Solomon	Song	Acts	Acts

Climbing Up

Romans	Rom.	Titus	Titus
1 Corinthians	1 Cor.	Philemon	Phm.
2 Corinthians	2 Cor.	Hebrews	Heb.
Galatians	Gal.	James	Js.
Ephesians	Eph.	1 Peter	1 Pet.
Philippians	Phil.	2 Peter	2 Pet.
Colossians	Col.	1 John	1 Jn.
1 Thessalonians	1 Thess.	2 John	2 Jn.
2 Thessalonians	2 Thess.	3 John	3 Jn.
1 Timothy	1 Tim.	Jude	Jude
2 Timothy	2 Tim.	Revelation	Rev.

Endnotes

[1] Scott Stroud, *Get Out for Good: A Practical Guide for Released Prisoners and Their Families* (Salinas: Cornerstone Books 2020), 23.

[2] Keith Phillips, *Out of Ashes* (Los Angeles: World Impact Press 1996), 98-99.

[3] Ibid., 102-103.

[4] Prison Fellowship Online Training Module *Prison Culture: A Prisoner's World*, 2012.

[5] Mark Walker, Cultural Exegesis (Gateway Seminary 2016), 5.

[6] Stanton E. Samenow, *Inside the Criminal Mind: Revised and Updated Edition* (New York: Broadway Books 2014). 3.

[7] Ibid. 113.

[8] Mark Walker, Cultural Exegesis (Gateway Seminary 2016), 5.

[9] https://www.prisonfellowship.org/resources/training-resources/in-prison/on-going-ministry/criminogenic-needs-risk-returning-prison/?utm_source=NEWS&utm_medium=EMAIL&utm_campaign=PF-AWR&utm_term=NEWS&utm_content=risks%20of%20recidivism&spMailingID=17753810&spUserID=MTI0MjkyMzYwNzk0S0&spJobID=1062106038&spReportId=MTA2MjEwNjA-zOAS2]

[10] Prison Fellowship Online Training Module *Prison Culture, Module 3: Recognizing Criminal Thinking*, 2012. Also see Lennie Spitale, *Prison Ministry: Understanding Prison Culture Inside and Out* (Nashville: Broadman & Holman Publishers 2002), 251-258.

[11] Mark Walker, "They Were All Afraid of Him: Former Prisoners and the Local Church," *Tameonta* Vol 6 No 2, (September 2019), 3-5.

[12] Lennie Spitale, *Prison Ministry: Understanding Prison Culture Inside and Out* (Nashville: Broadman & Holman Publishers 2002), 252.

[13] Alicia Chole, *Anonymous: Jesus' Hidden Years...and Yours* (Nashville: Thomas Nelson 2006), Kindle location 1141.

[14] https://www.prisonfellowship.org/resources/training-resources/in-prison/on-going-ministry/criminogenic-needs-risk-returning-prison/?utm_source=NEWS&utm_medium=EMAIL&utm_campaign=PF-AWR&utm_term=NEWS&utm_content=risks%20of%20recidivism&spMailingID=17753810&spUserID=MTI0MjkyMzYwNzk0S0&spJobID=1062106038&spReportId=MTA2MjEwNjA-zOAS2]

[15] Ibid.

[16] Dallas Willard, *The Divine Conspiracy* (New York: HarperCollins Publishers 1998), 329.

[17] Don Davis, *Capstone Curriculum, Module #6, God the Father* (Wichita: The Urban Ministry Institute 2005), 5-6.

[18] Dallas Willard, *The Divine Conspiracy* (New York: HarperCollins Publishers 1998), 338.

Climbing Up

[19] Ibid., 62.

[20] A.W. Tozer, *The Divine Conquest* (Jilliby: Living Book Press 1995), 51.

[21] C.S. Lewis, *Mere Christianity* (New York: Macmillan Publishing Co. 1952), 46.

[22] William Backus and Marie Chapian, *Telling Yourself the Truth* (Bloomington: Bethany House Publishers 2000), 65.

[23] Gordon Fee, Paul, The Spirit, and the People of God (Grand Rapids: Baker Books Publisher 2013), 127.

[24] Ibid., 168.

[25] Alicia Chole, *Anonymous: Jesus' Hidden Years...and Yours* (Nashville: Thomas Nelson 2006), Kindle location 1098.

[26] Caroline Leaf, *Switch On Your Brain* (Grand Rapids: Baker Books Publisher 2013).

[27] Neil Anderson, *Victory over the Darkness* (Ventura: Regal Books 1990), 163.

[28] Richard Foster and James Bryan Smith, eds., *Devotional Classics* (New York: HarperCollins Publishers 1990), 182.

[29] Unless otherwise noted, all quotes and references regarding the Lewis and Clark story are from *Undaunted Courage* by Stephen Ambrose (New York: Simon and Schuster 1996).

[30] Stanton E. Samenow, *Inside the Criminal Mind: Revised and Updated Edition* (New York: Broadway Books 2014), 306.

[31] Ken Burns, Lewis and Clark: The Journey of the Corps of Discovery (Burbank: PBS Home Video 1997).

[32] James Charlton, ed., *The Military Quotation Book* (New York: St. Martin's Press 2002), 12.

[33] Bill Gothard, *Institute for Basic Youth Conflicts* (Oak Brook: Institute for Basic Youth Conflicts 1979), 150-151.

[34] Ibid., 149-150.

[35] Todd Bolsinger, *Canoeing the Mountains: Christian Leadership in Uncharted Territory* (Downers Grove: IVP 2018), xx.

[36] George Ladd, *The Gospel of the Kingdom* (Grand Rapids: Eerdmans 1959).

[37] John White, *The Fight* (Downers Grove: IVP, 1976), 154.

[38] Henry Blackaby and Claude King, *Experiencing God* (Nashville: LifeWay Press 1990).

[39] Richard Foster and James Bryan Smith, eds., *Devotional Classics* (New York: HarperCollins Publishers 1990).

[40] Insight and Outlook. November 1996. The New Science of Leadership: An interview with Margaret Wheatley. http://www.scottlondon.com/insight/scripts/wheatley.html.

[41] Welch, Jack. September 2005. The Five Stages of Crisis Management. Opinion Journal. www.opinion.journal.com/editorial/feature.html?id=110007256.

[42] James Charlton, ed., *The Military Quotation Book* (New York: St. Martin's Press 2002), 5.

[43] http://www.climbingtechniques.org/basic-moves.html

Endnotes

Fred Nelson, *Spiritual Survival Guide: For Prison and Beyond* (Park Ridge: The Inside Out Network 2012), 175.

45 Neil Anderson, *Victory over the Darkness* (Ventura: Regal Books 1990), 52-53.

46 Dallas Willard, *The Divine Conspiracy* (New York: HarperCollins Publishers 1998), 353-360.

47 JP Moreland, *The God Question* (Eugene: Harvest House Publisher 2009), 203-204. J. P. Moreland talks about golf but the same principle applies.

48 Ibid.

49 Don L. Davis, *Compelling Testimony: Maintaining a Disciplined Walk, Christlike Character, and Godly Relationships as God's Servant* (Wichita: The Urban Ministry Institute 2006).

50 Timothy Jennings, *The God-Shaped Brain: How Changing Your View of God Transforms Your Life* (Downers Grove: InterVarsity Press 2013), 58.

51 Richard Foster and James Bryan Smith, eds., *Devotional Classics* (New York: HarperCollins Publishers 1990), 154.

Made in the USA
Middletown, DE
29 August 2023

37496378R00156